FLOYD CLYMER'S MOTORCYCLIST'S LIBRARY

The Book of the
SUNBEAM

A COMPLETELY ILLUSTRATED AND
PRACTICAL GUIDE FOR OWNERS OF
1928–1939 MODELS

BY
LESLIE K. HEATHCOTE

REVISED BY
W. C. HAYCRAFT, F.R.S.A

ANNOUNCEMENT

By special arrangement with the original publishers of this book, Sir Isaac Pitman & Son, Ltd., of London, England, we have secured the exclusive publishing rights for this book, as well as all others in THE MOTORCYCLIST'S LIBRARY.

Included in THE MOTORCYCLIST'S LIBRARY are complete instruction manuals covering the care and operation of respective motorcycles and engines; valuable data on speed tuning, and thrilling accounts of motorcycle race events. See listing of available titles elsewhere in this edition.

We consider it a privilege to be able to offer so many fine titles to our customers.

FLOYD CLYMER
Publisher of Books Pertaining to Automobiles and Motorcycles
2125 W. PICO ST.   LOS ANGELES 6, CALIF.

INTRODUCTION

Welcome to the world of digital publishing ~ the book you now hold in your hand, while unchanged from the original edition, was printed using the latest state of the art digital technology. The advent of print-on-demand has forever changed the publishing process, never has information been so accessible and it is our hope that this book serves your informational needs for years to come. If this is your first exposure to digital publishing, we hope that you are pleased with the results. Many more titles of interest to the classic automobile and motorcycle enthusiast, collector and restorer are available via our website at www.VelocePress.com. We hope that you find this title as interesting as we do.

NOTE FROM THE PUBLISHER

The information presented is true and complete to the best of our knowledge. All recommendations are made without any guarantees on the part of the author or the publisher, who also disclaim all liability incurred with the use of this information.

TRADEMARKS

We recognize that some words, model names and designations, for example, mentioned herein are the property of the trademark holder. We use them for identification purposes only. This is not an official publication.

INFORMATION ON THE USE OF THIS PUBLICATION

This manual is an invaluable resource for the classic motorcycle enthusiast and a "must have" for owners interested in performing their own maintenance. However, in today's information age we are constantly subject to changes in common practice, new technology, availability of improved materials and increased awareness of chemical toxicity. As such, it is advised that the user consult with an experienced professional prior to undertaking any procedure described herein. While every care has been taken to ensure correctness of information, it is obviously not possible to guarantee complete freedom from errors or omissions or to accept liability arising from such errors or omissions. Therefore, any individual that uses the information contained within, or elects to perform or participate in do-it-yourself repairs or modifications acknowledges that there is a risk factor involved and that the publisher or its associates cannot be held responsible for personal injury or property damage resulting from the use of the information or the outcome of such procedures.

WARNING!

One final word of advice, this publication is intended to be used as a reference guide, and when in doubt the reader should consult with a qualified technician.

PREFACE

SINCE the original edition of *The Book of the Sunbeam* was first published in 1933, there have been, of course, various detail changes in models and specifications, but the basic qualities of superb workmanship and finish, together with material of the highest quality, have remained unchanged. These excellent qualities were enhanced by the makers of the Matchless, who acquired the Sunbeam concern prior to World War II.

Since the war the manufacture of Sunbeam motor-cycles by Messrs. Matchless Motor Cycles has ceased and is now undertaken by Messrs. Sunbeam Cycles, Ltd. of Birmingham, 11 (Proprietors, B.S.A. Cycles, Ltd.). All single-cylinder Sunbeams have been discontinued by this firm, and production is now concentrated exclusively on two luxurious all-weather spring frame models of beautiful appearance. These two machines are powered with 500 c.c. monobloc overhead-camshaft engines. Shaft drive is an attractive feature of their specification. When more of them are available for the home market and are in use on the roads of the U.K., it is hoped to deal with them in this handbook. In the meantime the *present edition covers earlier Sunbeam models of 1928-39 vintage*. Oil, sparking plug recommendations, etc., have been brought fully up to date.

What about spare parts for the earlier John Marston Sunbeams? Owners of such models may be interested to know that Messrs. B. G. England of London Road, Dunstable, Beds. (Telephone: Dunstable 843-4) keep substantial stocks of motor-cycle and engine spares. This firm should be able to help you when trouble arises.

In conclusion the writer wishes you trouble-free running, and maximum m.p.g. at minimum expense. It is hoped that this handbook will help you to attain these objectives.

CONTENTS

CHAP.		PAGE
I.	DRIVING	1
II.	LUBRICATION	19
III.	THE ENGINE	27
IV.	GEAR-BOX AND CLUTCH	52
V.	COMPONENTS	67
VI.	ELECTRICAL SYSTEMS	88
VII.	COMPETITIONS AND COMPETITION WORK	104
VIII.	OVERHAULING	114
	INDEX	124

INSET

FIGS. 45B AND 45C. WIRING DIAGRAMS 90

CHAPTER I
DRIVING

It is somewhat rare to find a novice purchasing a Sunbeam on which to serve his "apprenticeship." Rather it is a machine which is the culminating ambition of many riders. However, for the benefit of those whose motto is "The best is the cheapest in the long run" and who commence their motor-cycling days on a Sunbeam, this chapter will materially assist them in putting the machine on the road.

Generally speaking, the prospective purchaser will find that the motor-cycle agent whom he approaches is only too willing to fix up all the preliminary formalities, but the following will enable him to carry them out himself if need be.

Driving Licence. Every driver of a motor-cycle must carry a driving licence, which is obtained (Form DLI) from the local County Council. The fee payable for it is 5s. and the licence is valid for one year. This enables him to drive any motor-cycle or car, providing he is seventeen years of age, or over. Always carry your licence on your person as it will be found invaluable in the case of an accident, and must be produced to police on demand. The licence must be signed immediately on receipt.

Insurance. With the introduction of the Road Traffic Act of 1930, it is essential that a third party insurance, at least, must be taken out before the registration disk can be obtained. In the case of a fairly expensive new machine, it is advisable to take out a full comprehensive insurance policy, and the cost of this for a 500 c.c. machine is very reasonable.

Insure only with a first-class insurance company and when filling in the proposal form, answer every question. Any false statements or misrepresentations might enable the insurance company to render the policy invalid.

A certificate of insurance is issued by the insurance company and it is advisable to carry this on the person as in the case of the driving licence. However, the regulations permit the production of the certificate and/or driving licence at the nearest police station within a period of five days.

Although it may not appear so at first sight, insurance is undoubtedly the best of safeguards. Accidents will happen, and how many could afford to pay damages amounting to perhaps a thousand pounds? This might occur if one were unfortunate enough to knock down and severely injure a pedestrian.

Armed with the certificate of insurance, the next procedure is to obtain the registration disk. This, in the case of a new machine, or upon a change of hands, requires Form R.F. 1/2 to be filled up. If it is just a matter of renewing the licence, use Form R.F. 1/A. Both the above forms are available at the County Council's offices and at any head post office. Motor-cycles, similarly to cars, are taxed on horse-power, the annual duty payable in the case of 250 c.c., 350 c.c., and 500 c.c. Sunbeams being £1 17s. 6d., and £3 15s., and £3 15s. respectively. If the machine is to be used with sidecar, a further 25s. per annum will be necessary. The licensing authorities, however, having compunction on the sometimes impecunious motor-cyclist, will allow the tax to be paid quarterly, which works out at £1 0s. 8d. for a 350–500 c.c. solo and £1 7s. 7d. for a sidecar. The licence disk, which is obtained when the appropriate fee has been paid, must be affixed to the machine in a conspicuous position on the near side in front of the saddle. The usual position is on the near-side of the front forks.

Driving Tests. It is to-day legally necessary for the prospective rider to undergo a test for competency before he is allowed to obtain a driving licence, and will be compelled to pass the test before a driving licence is granted. The necessary qualifications in order to pass the test are as follows—

(1) That he is fully conversant with the highway code.
(2) That he has ability unaided to—
  (a) Start the engine of the vehicle.
  (b) Move away straight ahead or at an angle.
  (c) Overtake, meet, or cross the path of other vehicles and take an appropriate course.
  (d) Turn right-hand and left-hand corners correctly.
  (e) Stop the vehicle in an emergency or normally, and in the latter case bring the vehicle to rest at an appropriate part of the road.
  (f) Give by hand (except in the case of a disabled driver) and by mechanical means (if fitted to the vehicle) in a clear and unmistakable manner, appropriate signals at appropriate times to indicate his intended actions; and act promptly on all signals given by traffic signs, traffic controllers, and other road users.
(3) That generally he is capable of driving a motor vehicle of the particular class to which the application relates without danger to other users of the road.

There is also a test in ability to reverse, but this will not be of interest to the motor-cyclist.

The person submitting himself for test will be required to provide his own machine, and will be required to pay the Government inspector conducting the test a fee of 10s. Upon passing the test he will receive a certificate. Provisional licences (cost is 5s.) (Form DLI) for those learning to ride are valid for three months. Learners are required to carry "L" plates back and front, and they are strictly forbidden to carry a passenger until the driving test has been passed. When ready for a driving test, fill up form DL 26.

Registration Book. With every new machine registered a book is supplied by the County Council, giving all particulars of the machine; date of original registration; cubic capacity, etc.

The idea of this is to prevent the sale of the machine in the event of it being stolen. Never purchase a secondhand machine unless the registration book is produced.

The book should be put into a safe place, as it need only be produced as follows—

1. On demand by a police officer or local taxation officer.
2. When renewing the tax.
3. On change of address.
4. If any alterations are made necessitating an increase on the tax paid—i.e. attachment of sidecar.
5. If the machine is sent permanently out of Great Britain or broken up.

Number Plates. There are various types of number plates on the market. Probably the neatest are the cast aluminium type and these are cast to standard size. The following will assist those who either paint the numbers or use transfer letters—

The figures and numbers on the front plate must be $1\frac{3}{4}$ in. deep; $1\frac{1}{4}$ in. wide and $\frac{5}{16}$ in. thick. For the rear, the dimensions are as follows: $2\frac{1}{2}$ in. high; $\frac{3}{8}$ in. broad and the total width of the space taken by every letter must be $1\frac{3}{4}$ in., except in the case of the figure 1. The space between adjoining letters and between adjoining figures must be $\frac{1}{2}$ in., and there must be a margin between the nearest part of any letter or figure and the top and bottom of the black surface upon which the identification mark is inscribed of at least $\frac{1}{2}$ in. The law requires that the rear plate must be effectively illuminated.

Lamps. In practically all cases it will be found that an efficient electric lighting set is fitted as standard. This will no doubt be found to comply with the requirements of the authorities—that a white light to the front and a red light to the rear must be shown during the hours of darkness, which are defined as under—

(*a*) As regards the period of summer-time—the time between one hour after sunset and one hour before sunrise.

(*b*) As regards the remainder of the year—the time between half an hour after sunset and half an hour before sunrise.

A sidecar machine must also be fitted with a white light on the sidecar to indicate the entire width of the outfit. It is, perhaps, not generally known that spotlights, which are frequently fitted by enthusiastic owners, must not be alight when the machine is in motion as this is contrary to the regulations. A very useful addition to the headlamp is a fog disk. This can be purchased very cheaply at an accessory firm and will prove of immense value if the machine is used much in foggy weather.

Horn. All motor vehicles must carry a horn in order to give audible warning of approach and the choice lies between a good-class bulb horn or the now almost universal electric pattern.

Use the horn as sparingly as possible. It is often quite easy to slip unobtrusively past when an ear-splitting blast on the horn would cause pedestrians to lose their nerve and an accident ensue. Do not, when stationary or between 11.30 p.m. and 7 a.m. sound the horn, except to avoid an accident.

Noise. The Sunbeam has always been noted for its extreme silence, but even so, it is possible to drive in such a way as to cause excessive noise. Nothing causes the motor-cyclist to be viewed with more disfavour than a noisy machine, so avoid tampering with the silencing system like the plague. Removing baffle plates or drilling holes in the silencers, although they may appear "sporty," only ensure that the rider will be convicted in the event of a police prosecution. Allowing the exhaust to emit a terrific roar whilst in the vicinity of institutions such as hospitals, churches, etc., is not only the worst of taste but brings down the vituperation of all intelligent citizens.

Riding Kit. A few words on the clothes used when motor-cycling will not be amiss and it is proposed to deal with the various garments suitable for different weather conditions.

For the all-the-year-round rider who encounters really bad rainstorms, there can be no doubt but that Hutchinson waders and a poncho are the best protection. Accompanied by a scarf wrapped round the neck, the rider should survive the fiercest of storms if wearing the above-mentioned articles. Many riders favour the black rubber competition coat in place of the poncho, and this certainly has some advantages, notably in the matter of pockets. In cold, windy weather, a leather coat is a useful adjunct as there is nothing like leather for keeping the wind out, and this, coupled with a pair of waterproof leggings, should prove quite suitable for short journeys.

The rider who wishes to enter his Sunbeam for competitive events, such as speed trials, grass track racing, trials, etc., will find that leather breeches, a leather jerkin, and field boots the most suitable, as these garments give plenty of warmth and do not restrict the freedom which is essential in sporting events.

A very useful accessory for the everyday rider is a pair of handlebar muffs. These are obtainable for about 10s. and will prove invaluable in really cold weather.

It will be found that a pair of goggles will enable the rider to cover a much greater distance without feeling tired, and these should be of the best quality, fitted with unsplinterable glass. At all costs avoid cheap goggles fitted with ordinary glass and if a good pair is beyond one's purse, a pair of celluloid ones obtained from any of the well-known stores are the best substitute.

Clubs. The new owner will be well advised to join the local motor-cycling club. This is very useful, inasmuch as it brings the rider into contact with a number of cheery fellows, only too willing to assist in any difficulty. The benefits of club life are manifold, including competitive events such as trials, grass tracks, social events, dances, etc. Most clubs possess a club house wherein the members gather several times a week and discuss the various machines and their points. All this will be found very helpful to the beginner.

For those to whom club life has no appeal, the author would recommend the joining of one of the big road organizations—the R.A.C. or the A.A. The address of the Royal Automobile Club (Associate Section) is 85 Pall Mall, S.W.1, and that of the Automobile Association, Fanum House, New Coventry Street, W.1. The subscription to either of these organizations is a small sum per annum for which a large number of privileges are conferred. Amongst the latter may be numbered a "Get-you-Home-Service," free legal advice, assistance if in trouble on the road, use of telephone boxes which are located at the road-side, advice with regard to touring, both at home and abroad and the supplying of itineraries.

Running-in. The Sunbeam, not being a mass-production machine, is turned out by the makers with all the moving parts fitted as near to perfection as possible, but it behoves every new owner to treat his machine gently for the first thousand miles. It is recommended that 10 miles per hour in bottom, 18 in second, 25 in third, and 30 miles per hour in top should not be exceeded for the first 500 miles. During the following 500 miles, these speeds may be increased by, roughly, 5 to 10 miles per hour, depending upon which gear is in use. If small throttle openings are maintained and the engine is kept well supplied with oil, the bearing surfaces should have every opportunity of bedding down nicely. The main object is to keep the machine from labouring unduly, i.e. ascending a hill at 25 miles per hour in second gear will place more stress on the engine than descending the same hill at 40 miles per hour in top gear. The running-in period is a very trying one. To be passed by the rider of an ancient two-stroke is very galling, but refrain from opening out and giving chase and you will congratulate yourself upon your abstinence in this respect at a later date. It will do no harm to open up for short periods after the 1,000 mile mark has been passed, but the throttle should not be kept wide for any length of time and immediately shut down if the engine shows any sign of running tight or drying up. These occasional bursts of speed are useful, as they will indicate any "high spots" on the piston. "High spots" will be referred to later on.

Driving Tactics. The main control on the machine is the throttle, and the speed should be regulated by this as far as possible, supplemented by an occasional application of the brakes. Get to know how long the machine takes to slow up by simply throttling down. Try and use the brakes as sparingly as possible. Violent deceleration by means of harsh application of the brakes takes its toll in excessive tyre wear, chain and sprocket renewals, etc. The really expert driver seldom finds it necessary to apply his brakes fiercely. He is on the alert and is able to decrease his speed by means of the throttle.

A most pernicious practice and one to be absolutely condemned, which is sometimes indulged in by the inexperienced rider, is that of lifting the exhaust lever to slow down. The exhaust valve lifter is for starting purposes only, and using it when the machine is in motion will cause the exhaust valve to distort and burn out.

Use of Clutch. The object of the clutch is to enable the drive from the engine to the gear-box to be gradually taken up and also to assist in changing gear. Do not ill-treat the clutch by undue slipping. It must not be slipped to assist the machine in cornering or climbing hills, otherwise it may burn out. The gear-box is there to be used and far less strain is placed on the machine by changing down to a lower gear. Avoid holding the clutch "out" too long when in a traffic block; it is far better to get into neutral.

Braking. Generally speaking, it is advisable to use the brakes in conjunction. The front one should be applied gently, slightly after the rear one has been brought into operation. There is a period just before the wheel locks at which braking power is at its maximum, and the rider should get to know when this occurs. Do not apply the front brake hard, independently, when the roads are greasy, if you wish to avoid front wheel skids.

Cornering. Correct cornering methods are largely a matter of experience. Remember to use the throttle and apply the brakes before the corner is reached. This method of approach, besides being neater, enables the rider to use the brakes really hard if some obstacle is encountered on the bend. Bear in mind that it does *not* take two to cause a smash. Always assume that the "other fellow" will be passing a slower vehicle on the wrong side, occupying your half of the road, and you will then be in a position to do the right thing. Exercise the utmost caution at cross road and blind corners. Do not give a sharp blast on the horn and sweep majestically past without decreasing speed. Someone else may also think they are on the main road. When turning into a side road, give the oncoming traffic ample warning. Suddenly switching off the main road with just a half-hearted waggle of the hand is often the cause of hard words. Hump-backed bridges should be treated cautiously. The manner in which the machine leaves the ground at the top may be very exhilarating, but this may have to be paid for very dearly if something should happen to be coming in the opposite direction.

The handling of a sidecar on corners is entirely different from a solo, inasmuch as a sidecar is driven and not ridden round. The inexperienced rider will do well to carry a passenger or ballast in the sidecar, otherwise there will be tendency for the sidecar to lift if a left-hand bend is taken too fast. In the event of this occurring, the best method is to steer to the right and open the throttle slightly. The correct procedure for taking left-hand bends is as follows: Reduce the speed by means of the throttle *before* the corner is reached and accelerate slightly as the outfit rounds the bend. This method enables the outfit to pivot on the sidecar wheel. The opposite applies when taking a right-hand bend. Close the throttle and apply the rear brake. This allows the sidecar to run round the machine, the pivoting action then taking place on the rear wheel of the motor-cycle. The main thing is to keep to a moderate speed on left-hand corners until complete confidence in the handling of the outfit is obtained. The author has ridden a sidecar outfit with the sidecar wheel in the air for quite a considerable time. It is just a question of balance.

" Driving " and " Riding." Although these terms may appear to be almost synonymous, in practice there is a vast difference. *Driving* entails merely using the machine as a conveyance, controlling it in a wooden and unintelligent fashion. When driving a sidecar outfit (for practical purposes a three-wheeler) the question of balance ordinarily does not enter the picture, and it is impossible to ride it in the real sense of the word as one can a solo mount. Solo mounts are very manoeuvrable.

The man who rides his machine uses his faculties of balance and intelligence and learns the tricks and whims of his machine, thus enabling him to blend the machine and himself into one. He cultivates the "feel" of the machine until he becomes a "part" of it in a similar fashion to that of a good horseman who becomes part of his horse. Watch a famous T.T. rider taking Hilberry corner in the Isle of Man at perhaps 70 miles per hour or more; machine and rider swirl round at this colossal speed, as if one unit —a perfect combination of balance, coupled with experience.

The good rider never allows his machine to emit sounds of distress through hanging on in top gear too long. He delights in making those early changes, quick and clean, which are the envy of his less fortunate brethren. Be a good master and the machine will also be a good servant.

Pillion Riding. It is not advisable for the beginner to carry a pillion passenger until he has become well acquainted with the machine. A large number of accidents are ascribed by the "Scare Press" to pillion riding, but most of this is sheer rubbish. Pillion riding can be and is as safe as any other form of transport. The regulations now require that a proper pillion seat be fixed and that the passenger should sit astride. The proper pillion is not clearly defined, but any of the popular patterns such as are obtainable to-day will be found quite suitable. See that a pair of pillion footrests are provided, not only for the comfort of the passenger, but also for the peace of mind of the driver. There is nothing more annoying than a passenger who is continually fidgeting about, upsetting the stability of the machine, with the added danger of the possibility of getting entangled with the transmission or the back wheel. The driver should avoid sudden swerves and striking large pot-holes at speed. *He* may be ready, but the passenger cannot always be expected to see them.

Skidding. "They skid terribly" is a remark heard, generally aired by a non-motorist, and it is these kind of remarks that cause

Fig. 1. Important Road Signs to Observe
(Reproduced by courtesy of H.M.S.O.)

the novice rider many uneasy thoughts. These ideas are absolutely erroneous. True, it *is* possible to make a machine skid, but only under great provocation. Probably the greatest curse to the motor-cyclist are greasy tramlines. Fortunately, these are now superseded in most districts by trolley buses.

A few anti-skidding hints are given herewith: (1) The best way to deal with greasy tramlines is to cross them fairly slowly at a wide angle. (2) Drive a little slower than your general average speed, that is to say, if your usual speed is 40 miles per hour, cut this speed down to 35 miles per hour. This inspires confidence. (3) Never apply the rear brake hard and de-clutch at the same time. This is almost bound to invoke rear wheel skids. (4) Dump those old worn-out tyres on the scrap heap. The price of a pair of tyres is cheap compared with one's life. (5) Avoid banking the machine over too much on a corner; take it a little slower and almost vertically. (6) Find a nice, quiet section of road and practise skidding deliberately, or, alternatively, the trials course provides an excellent practising ground; this has the added advantage that mud is a nice, soft landing place. (7) Wherever possible, steer into the skid to bring the machine under control. (8) Change down to a lower gear in order that the engine may turn over freely. The most important thing is to remain calm and unflurried. Immunity from side slip is largely a matter of nerves.

Hand Signals. All signals given should be made at a time when the following traffic has ample opportunity to act on them. Last minute hand-wagging is worse than useless. When turning right, a quick glance over the shoulder is the best safeguard as occasionally a hand signal may not be understood. Needless to say, the signals given by self-appointed traffic controllers should be ignored. In the event of an accident these well-intentioned people would no doubt disclaim all responsibility, thus leaving the onus on you.

The correct hand signals which should be used by all motor-cyclists are as follows—

(*a*) *To Indicate Intention to Turn Right.* Extend the right arm and hand, with the palm turned to the front, and keep them horizontal and rigid.

(*b*) *To Indicate Intention to Turn Left.* Extend the right arm and hand straight from the shoulder and rotate slowly in an anti-clockwise direction. Alternatively, extend the left arm.

(*c*) *To Indicate Intention to Stop or Slow Down.* Extend the right arm, with the palm of the hand downwards, and move the arm slowly up and down, keeping the wrist loose.

(*d*) *To Indicate Intention to Desire to be Overtaken.* Extend the right arm and hand below the level of the shoulder and move them slowly backwards and forwards.

Road Signs. The various road signs depicted in Fig. 1 are erected at their appointed places in various parts of the country.

Some of the sketches are reproduced from "The Highway Code" by courtesy of H.M. Stationery Office. At the extreme right below the symbolic signs are shown the 30 m.p.h. general speed limit sign and the derestriction sign indicating that you can drive above 30 m.p.h., provided that your speed is not dangerous having regard to the existing circumstances. With regard to the "Major Road Ahead" signs, you must *stop* and not just slow down where the word "Halt" appears.

Fig. 2 shows the usual form of traffic lights. The warning sign is, however, generally omitted.

RED means "Stop" and wait *behind* the stop line.

RED AND AMBER means "Stop," but be prepared to start when *GREEN* shows.

AMBER means "Stop" at the stop line unless you have passed it, or are so close that stopping might cause an accident.

GREEN ARROW shown with *Red* indicates "Proceed in the direction of the arrow."

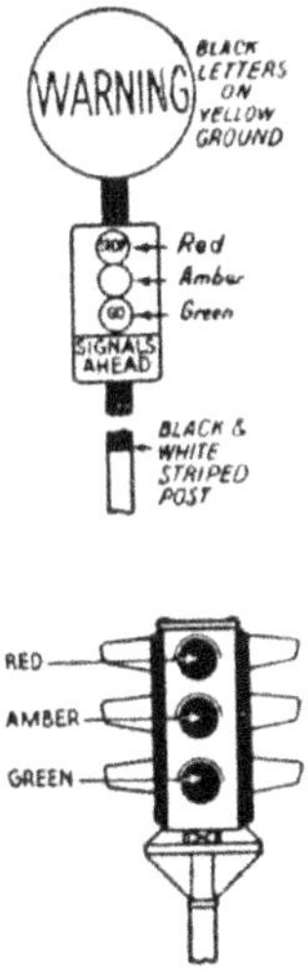

Speed Limit. The old question as to whether the imposition of a speed limit will decrease the number of road deaths again cropped up and from 18th March, 1935, it has been an offence to exceed 30 m.p.h. in a "built up area." A "built up area" is defined in the Act as a road in which a system of street lighting furnished by means of lamps placed not more than two hundred yards apart is provided. The local County Council can, however, apply to the Minister of Transport for permission to affix a speed limit sign to roads not coming in the above category.

Road Signs. The speed limit sign consists of a disk, 18 in. in diameter with "30" painted in black figures on a background of white and with an outer circle of red. Where no speed limit is in operation an 18 in. diameter disk with a black line across a white background is erected.

Pedestrian Crossings. These have been instituted for some years, and are marked by steel studs and black and white stripes placed at intervals across the road. To indicate some crossings a standard surmounted by a large yellow globe is placed on the pavement at each end. It behoves every motor-cyclist to go warily, as

FIG. 2
AUTOMATIC SIGNAL (BELOW) AND WARNING (ABOVE)
(*From "Road Sense,"* 1930)

summonses are being issued in cases where the pedestrian has not been allowed a free passage at a crossing.

Taking Delivery. Assuming the new owner is taking delivery of his machine, he will find the controls as in Fig. 3. Fig. 4 shows the controls of an earlier model. In some cases, especially on machines later than 1928, the throttle lever will be replaced by a twist-grip control, and usually the front brake is on the right-hand side and the exhaust lifter on the left.

On all the three-speed gear-box machines of the sliding pinion type, from 1921 to 1932, the gear positions are as Fig. 5. The

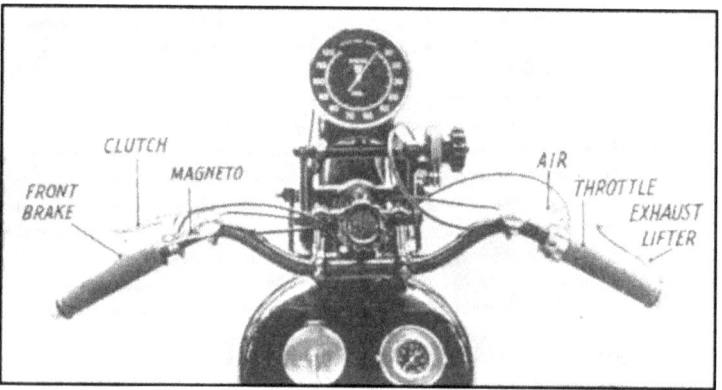

Fig. 3. The Controls (1932 Models)

other type, known as the cam-operated gear-box, is as Fig. 6. The bottom gear is in an exactly opposite position. This also applies to the 1932 four-speed gear-box. 1939 models have foot gear change.

Before attempting to start the engine up, it is as well to familiarize oneself with all the controls and in which direction they work, after which the engine may be started. The procedure is as follows.

Fill the petrol and oil tanks. Turn on petrol tap and depress carburettor tickler, open throttle lever $\frac{1}{6}$th to $\frac{1}{8}$th, and, using the exhaust lifter lever,* smartly depress the kick-starter. There is a certain knack in this which one acquires in time. The points to remember are, not to open the throttle lever too far and to release the exhaust valve lifter when the kick-starter has completed about two-thirds of its travel. On no account have the ignition lever more than one-half open. If this precaution is neglected, the kick-starter mechanism may be damaged

* On 1939 500 and 600 c.c. Lion S.V. models, do not forget first to raise the decompressor.

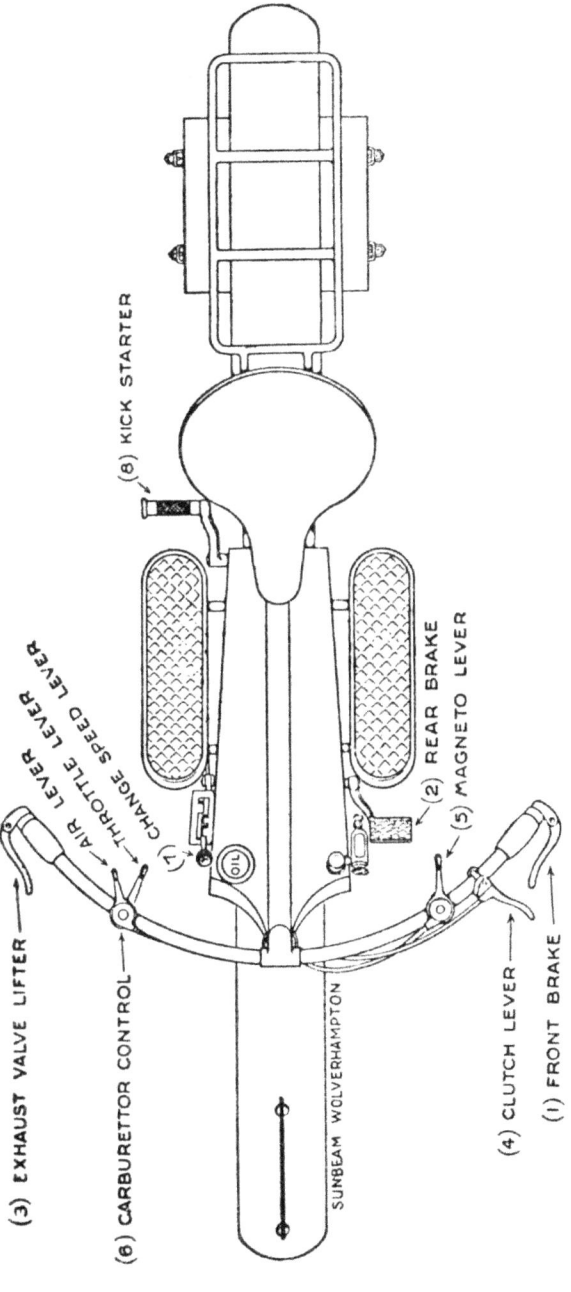

Fig. 4. The Controls (Early Models)

by the engine back-firing. Should the kick-starter not engage, or appear to stick, engage first gear and move the machine slightly, when it will free itself. Jumping on the kick-starter crank will only damage the ratchet pinion. When the engine has fired, open

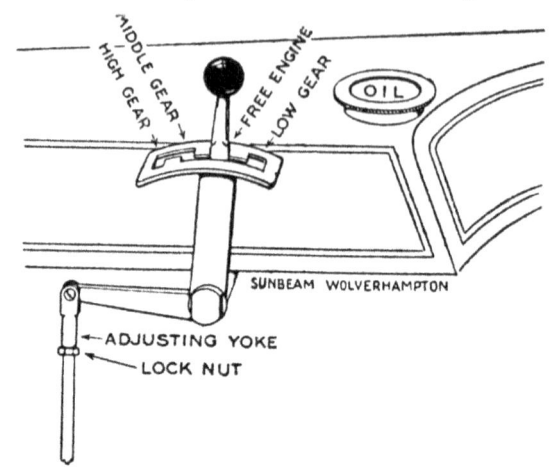

FIG. 5. GEAR LEVER (SLIDING PINION GEAR-BOX)

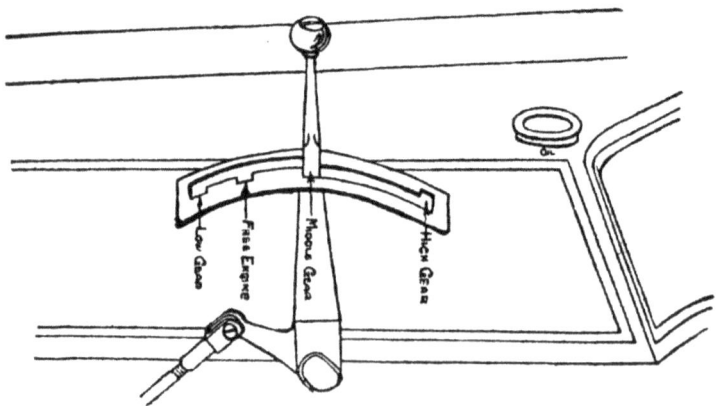

FIG. 6. GEAR LEVER (CAM-OPERATED GEAR-BOX)

the throttle lever slightly, and after the engine has run for a few minutes, the air lever may be opened fully and should remain so, except when starting from cold.

The engine is now running with the gear lever in neutral and, to start away, lift the clutch lever towards handlebar and move gear lever into first gear. If the clutch is gradually released and the throttle opened slightly at the same time, the machine will move away. If the machine jerks badly and stops, it is a fairly good indication that the clutch has been released too rapidly, so try again, bearing in mind that light use of the clutch lever is essential, and that it is the last quarter of travel that counts the most.

The machine is now on the move in first gear and opening the throttle until the machine has attained a fair speed, about 8 to 10 miles per hour, slightly close the throttle, release clutch lever, and move the gear lever into the second gear notch. Repeat this procedure when the machine has reached 25 to 30 miles per hour in second gear, only this time engaging top gear. On the four-speed gear-box it will be necessary to make one more change, that is from third into top. The expert driver's gear changes appear to the onlooker to be simply a variation in the engine note, and this should be the aim of every beginner. The machine is now travelling at a comfortable speed, about 30 to 35 miles per hour in top gear.

Changing down from a higher to a lower gear is a reverse of the above, i.e. de-clutch; open throttle slightly in order that the pinions in the gear-box and the road speed of the machine may correspond as near as possible; slip the gear lever into the lower position and release clutch. Generally speaking, it is advisable to allow the speed of the machine to get fairly low, but do not wait too long.

When changing down on a hill, do not allow the speed of the machine to get so low that it emits sounds of distress, generally known as "pinking." The change down should be made long before this.

General Driving. The driver will soon accustom himself to the feel of the various controls. Always keep the throttle in a position which gives the engine just enough to do the work in hand. An excess of gas will only waste petrol and make the machine run hot. Keep the magneto lever as far advanced as possible, only retarding the spark slightly on hills or for "tick-over."

Drive on the brakes as little as possible, and, if you cultivate this habit, you will be able to make a really quick stop in an emergency with the aid of the brakes. Harsh application of the brakes not only puts unnecessary stress on the machine but causes excessive tyre wear. Similarly, causing the engine to "rev" unnecessarily high on its intermediate gears causes rapid wear, and also attracts attention which is undesirable.

With the above tips and a few days on the road, if possible with an experienced friend, the new owner can now look forward to a season of enjoyment of one of the finest of sports.

Riding Position. To derive the utmost satisfaction from riding, the machine should be made as comfortable as possible. With this object in view the makers have endeavoured to cater for each individual taste by providing a wide scope for adjustment in the riding position.

(*a*) To raise or lower the saddle, slacken the nut on top of the seat pillar. (This does not apply to the Model 10.)

(*b*) To tilt the saddle up or down, or to adjust it backwards or forwards on the seat pillar, slacken the nuts at the end of the pins passing through the clip which attaches the saddle to the seat pillar.

(*c*) To adjust the handlebar, slacken the two pins on each of the clips which hold it. The handlebar can then be swung up or down enabling the height of the handlebar to be altered.

(*d*) The footrests can be set at varying points of a circle. Slacken the nuts at the end of the footrest rod and unscrew it two or three threads. The footrest brackets can then be drawn off the serrations and set at any desired position. The footrest pad itself can be set at any angle by slackening the nut at the end of the footrest bracket and giving it the desired twist. The foot-brake pedal may be adjusted to suit the footrest position by loosening the nut on the spindle which passes through the engine plates and turning the hexagon on the spindle to the required position.

Make good use of the wide range provided by these adjustments, as both comfort and control depend considerably upon the riding position being, so to speak, "tailor-made." Ride a considerable distance first with the riding position anyhow, and secondly with all the positions adjusted to suit the rider, and note the difference.

MAINTENANCE

One realizes, of course, that a new machine will have a bedding down process, and the following are a few of the minor adjustments necessary during the first 1,000 miles.

Adjusting Chains (Front). Slacken nut on oil-bath end of footrest rod, together with nuts holding gear-box to frame. To tighten chain, screw up draw-bolt adjuster until the chain has about $\frac{1}{4}$ in. sag, i.e. $\frac{1}{2}$ in. up-and-down movement.

This can be tested through the chain case inspection cover. Make sure that all the nuts are tightened up after this operation and check the adjustment again. A peculiar whining noise indicates that the chain is too tight; on the other hand, if it is allowed to get too loose it will knock on the chain case.

After adjusting front chain, always check the tension of the rear chain.

Rear. Slacken nut on left-hand side of pull-out spindle; slacken two $\frac{3}{4}$ in. large plated nuts on right-hand brake drum side. To tighten chain, screw in adjusters on each side of the machine, making sure that you give an equal number of turns, otherwise the wheel will be put out of alignment. A wheel gauge is provided for the latest machines, and this fits between the rim and the chain stay. The rear chain should be adjusted so that there is $\frac{1}{2}$ in. sag, i.e. 1 in. total up-and-down play. Tighten all nuts again securely and remember that tightening the nut on the pull-out spindle tightens the chain a little.

Magneto Chain. To adjust the magneto chain, slacken the two nuts on the studs holding magneto to platform (a special spanner is provided for this and will be referred to later). Slide the magneto on its platform, backwards to tighten, and re-tighten nuts. In the case of the magneto chain, the adjustment is about right when there is no appreciable sag in the chain, provided it is not rigid at its tightest point.

Tappets. To adjust the tappets on the side valve models, first remove the cover by unscrewing the large knurled knob. The inlet tappet should be adjusted so that there is scarcely any gap between the tappet head and the valve stem. At the most, the thickness of a cigarette paper is ample.

The exhaust should be adjusted to a clearance of $\frac{6}{1000}$ in. to $\frac{5}{1000}$ in. when cold. This clearance is about the thickness of the average visiting card. Loosen lock-nut and screw up head. Tighten lock-nut.

On the O.H.V. models, the tappet adjustment is effected at the end of the overhead rocker direct to the end of the valve stem.

The inlet tappet should be adjusted similar to that of the side valve, that is the thickness of a cigarette paper, while the exhaust should be $\frac{10}{1000}$ in. when cold. On the Model 90 as much as $\frac{12}{1000}$ in. may be allowed. See also page 123.

Brakes. The brake linings will tend to bed themselves down and these are easily adjusted by means of the knurled finger adjusters; the front one on the right-hand fork and the rear one on the right-hand rear stay. To take up the slack, turn in an anti-clockwise direction. This will be facilitated by applying the brake lever and pedal while the adjusters are screwed up.

When all the adjustment has been taken up, the brake-operating lever can be removed from the operating cam and moved to another serration. In order to do this, slacken the nut with washer, give the end of the cam a sharp blow with a hammer, and the cam lever may then be moved round.

Clutch Stops. Owing to the design of the gear-box, all Sunbeams are fitted with clutch stops in order to render gear changing easier.

As the corks on a new machine quickly bed themselves down, it may be found necessary to adjust the stops. These are located in the front chain case, and to adjust them slacken the large locknuts and screw in the adjusters until they touch the clutch plates. Then screw them back one and a quarter turns and tighten up the lock-nuts. If there is a grating noise when engaging first gear, it will probably be found that adjustment of the stops will cure this. The other cause of this difficulty is brought about by the clutch plates sticking and this may be cured as follows. It sometimes happens that too much oil gets into the front chain case, and in this event put in a squirtful of paraffin in the chain case. This will wash the oil off the clutch plates and enable them to work freely. The other tip is to depress the kick-starter several times with the clutch out before starting the engine. This is specially applicable to machines which have been standing for some time and where in all probability the oil on the clutch plates has congealed.

Cycle Parts. The front forks, hubs, and other small parts require greasing, and Tecalemit grease nipples are provided for this purpose. To lubricate these, fill the Tecalemit grease-gun by unscrewing the milled cap at nozzle, pushing down the cork inside the gun and filling from a tube of Castrolease light. Place the gun over the various nipples and give each a pump. Remember that "little and often" is the best motto. Give the hubs a quarter charge from the gun about every 500 miles. Too much lubricant at these points is to be avoided, as an excess may work through the hubs on to the brake linings and impair their efficiency.

The above covers most of what will be required to keep the machine in first-class trim during the running-in period, which is probably the most important in the life of the machine. Careful running-in may add years to the effective life of a machine.

CHAPTER II
LUBRICATION

CORRECT lubrication is a vital factor in the motor-cycle engine. Oil is its life-blood and, consequently, the various oiling systems used on Sunbeams since their inception will be explained as thoroughly as possible.

The object of oil is to interpose a film between two metal surfaces, such as a piston and cylinder, thus preventing them from touching and causing wear. Therefore it is most important to see that every part gets the lubricant it deserves, and this does not only include the main components, such as engine and gearbox, but all the minor parts that are frequently neglected, including Bowden cables; the various pivots of the gear control and brake mechanism; brake control wires and stand bolts. A drop of oil put on a bolt and nut in a second may save half an hour of struggling when the time comes to remove it.

Choice of Lubricants. Suitable engine oils for Sunbeams are Wakefields Castrol "Grand Prix" (XXL, winter), Shell X-100 SAE 50 (SAE 40, winter), Mobiloil D (BB, winter), Essolube Racer, and Price's Energol SAE 60. Naturally, the individual owner may wish to use his own particular brand of oil, but it is advisable to choose a first-class oil and stick to it. Continually changing will do no good.

"Castrol R" is recommended purely for racing or speed events, and to get the best out of this oil it is advisable to wash the tank and engine out after each meeting and refill the tank with fresh oil.

The early side-valve engines up to 1920 were fitted with a hand oil pump, as shown in Fig. 7. The object of this is to supply oil both to the gearbox and the engine. When the tap is turned down, as shown, the oil goes to the engine. The other pipe leads to the gear-box. For all normal running keep the tap pointing to the engine.

If the small catch holding the pump plunger is freed, the latter is free to rise and force oil through the drip feed. To regulate the speed at which the oil leaves the drip feed for the engine, turn the disk at the top, anti-clockwise to increase the rate of flow and clockwise to decrease it. It will be found that engines vary considerably in the amount of oil they require, but one pump about every eight miles is about right.

The crankcase should be drained out periodically, say about

every 1,000 miles, by means of the plug at the bottom of the crankcase. Then replace the plug and refill engine with five or six pumps. The draining off process will be facilitated if done at the end of a run when the engine is still warm.

Early Mechanical Pumps. The later side valve and earlier overhead valve models, i.e. those up to 1928, are fitted with mechanical oil pumps, situated outside the magneto chain cover. Some of these have auxiliary hand pumps as previously described. This pump is adjusted by loosening the two screws at the end and

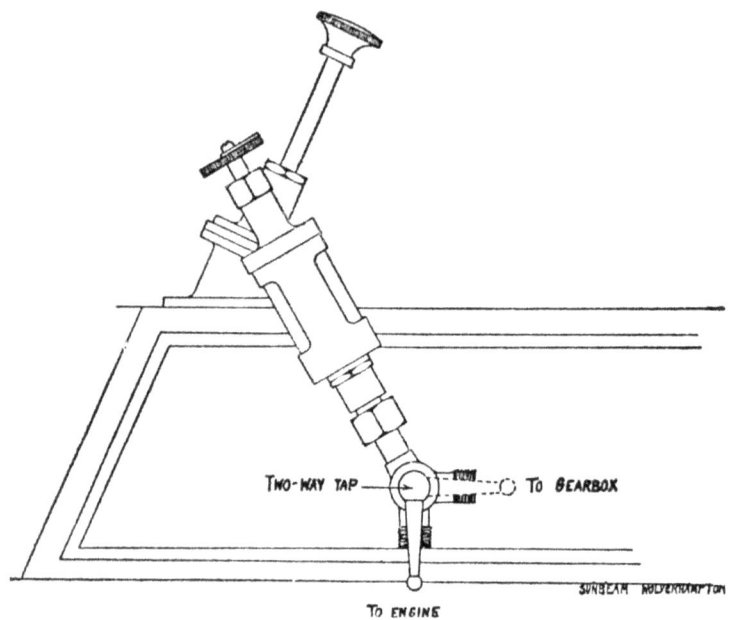

FIG. 7. TWO-WAY TAP

turning the regulator. About one-third to a half from the "off" position will be about right for all normal use.

1928 Machines, except Models 80 and 90. The mechanical pump on these machines is inside the magneto chain cover and the oil passes through a sight feed on the tank. With this system it is essential that the sight feed and pipe must be air tight. If the glass of the sight feed is broken at any time it must be replaced immediately, and if the pump has run dry it will be found necessary to fill the pump before it will again function properly. To do this, first fill the oil tank, remove the sight feed cap and glass and fill the delivery pipe with oil by means of an oil squirt. When the pipe is full, replace the cap and start the engine. The adjustment

LUBRICATION

for the pump is correct when the sight feed passes about thirty-forty drops per minute. For a really fast run this may, of course, be increased.

Dry Sump Lubrication. The 1929 and later $3\frac{1}{2}$ h.p. machines are fitted with dry sumps, and the system employed is illustrated in Fig. 8. On these machines the oil is in circulation all the time, and it is important that the oil in the tank should not drop below two-thirds full. The pump is set when the machine leaves the works and the only adjustment is provided by a regulator on the oil tank which controls the flow of oil into the pump. The knurled disk on the regulator has three positions, and to adjust it should be lifted up and turned round to the position required. Make sure that the hole in the disk and the peg in the body register correctly. The positions are as follows: No. 1, suitable for all ordinary running in medium weather; No. 2, suitable for long distance runs at a fast speed during warm weather; No. 3, passes the largest quantity of oil and is suitable for use in very cold weather when the oil is very thick, and also during the "running-in" period. The system itself functions automatically as soon as the engine is started. The tell-tale in the front connexion of the inner pump indicates when the system is working, the tell-tale being forced out. When the engine stops the tell-tale goes back and cuts off the oil flow. If the tell-tale does not come out when the engine is started, stop the engine and remove the tell-tale complete. Start the engine again and wait until the oil flows out of the tell-tale aperture. Stop the engine and replace tell-tale. Sometimes an airlock in the supply pipe may not be cleared in this way and, in this event, remove the supply pipe and charge it with oil. Oil should then be forced out of the tell-tale hole, when the tell-tale can be replaced. Should the tell-tale leak oil at any time, most probably the small leather washer in the tell-tale body is worn and requires renewing.

The dry sump system is very economical as a general rule, and the owner has no need to worry if it is found necessary to add a very small quantity of oil to the tank only at infrequent intervals. If the consumption appears excessive, the trouble is almost invariably due to worn or faulty piston rings.

1928 Models 80 and 90. A diagram of the system employed on these machines is shown in Fig. 9, and will bear explanation. On the Model 80, the pipe BB is led to the front of the crankcase from whence the oil is forced through the jet direct to the big end bearing. On the Model 90 it is led round the cylinder to a union over the right-hand engine shaft, the oil being led internally to the inside of the big end. The auxiliary oiling, which passes through pipe F and is operated by a lever similar to the clutch lever on

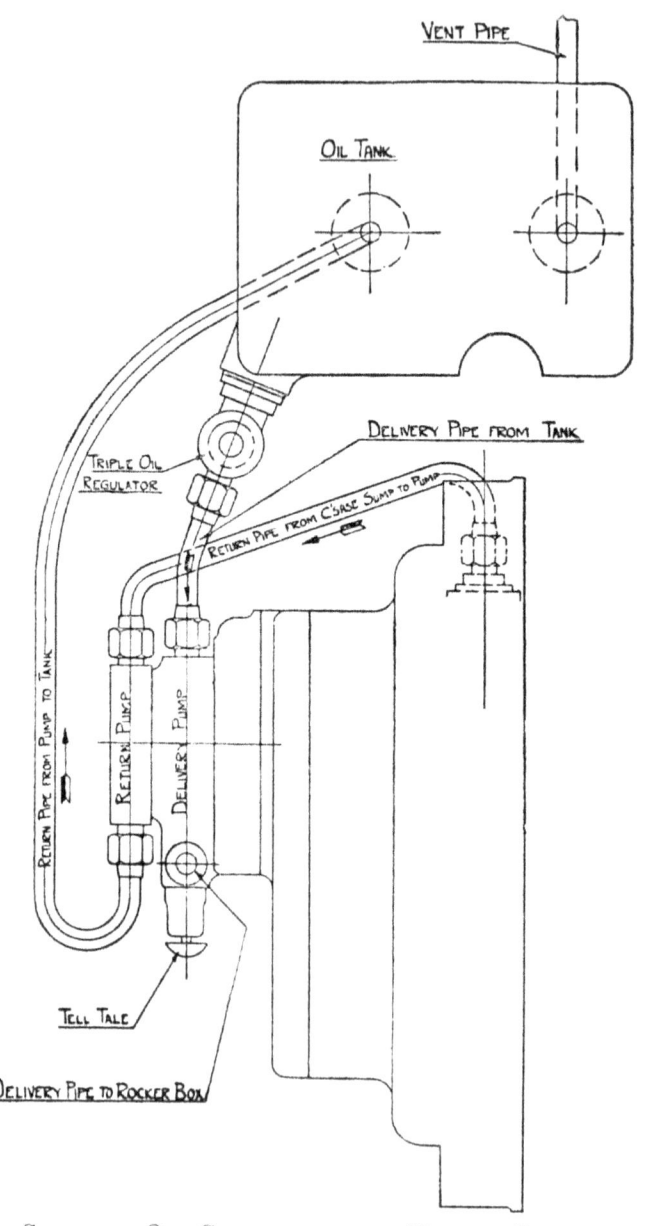

Fig. 8. Showing Oil Connexions on Models Lion, 9 and 90 (1929)

LUBRICATION

the handlebar, is not necessary for ordinary running, but it will be found useful for high speed touring.

As the oil is in constant circulation, forwards and backwards from tank to engine, it gradually loses its viscosity or lubricating properties. As long as the oil still has plenty of body, it is only

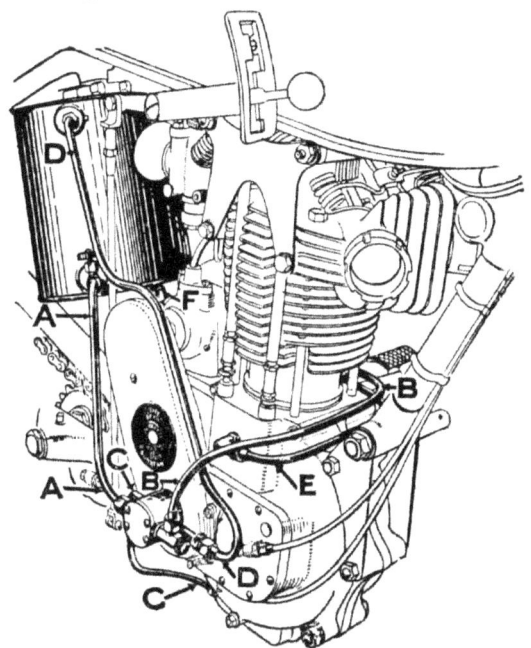

FIG. 9. OIL PIPE LAY-OUT (1928 DRY SUMP)

KEY TO FIG. 9

- *AA.* Supply pipe from regulator at base of oil tank to rearward connexion of outer pump.
- *BB.* Delivery pipe from tell-tale on front connexion of outer pump, supplying oil to big-end.
- *CC.* Extractor pipe from base of sump to rearward connexion of inner pump.
- *DD.* Return pipe from front connexion of inner pump to top of oil tank.
- *E.* Auxiliary pipe for additional oil, running from foot of hand-operated pump inside oil tank to connexion over timing gear.
- *F.* Vent pipe from union in base of oil tank to the atmosphere. This is to allow for escape of air pumped into the oil tank through *DD* together with the returned oil.

necessary to keep the oil at its normal level. When, however, the oil becomes thin and dirty from continual usage, it should be discarded and the tank refilled with fresh oil.

To empty the oil tank, remove the supply pipe; lean the machine well over to the right and hold a receptacle underneath to catch the oil. It is best to perform this operation when the oil is still warm, and to remove any foreign matter just swill the tank out with petrol or paraffin. The later machines (1929 and onwards) are fitted with filter gauzes and these should be cleaned

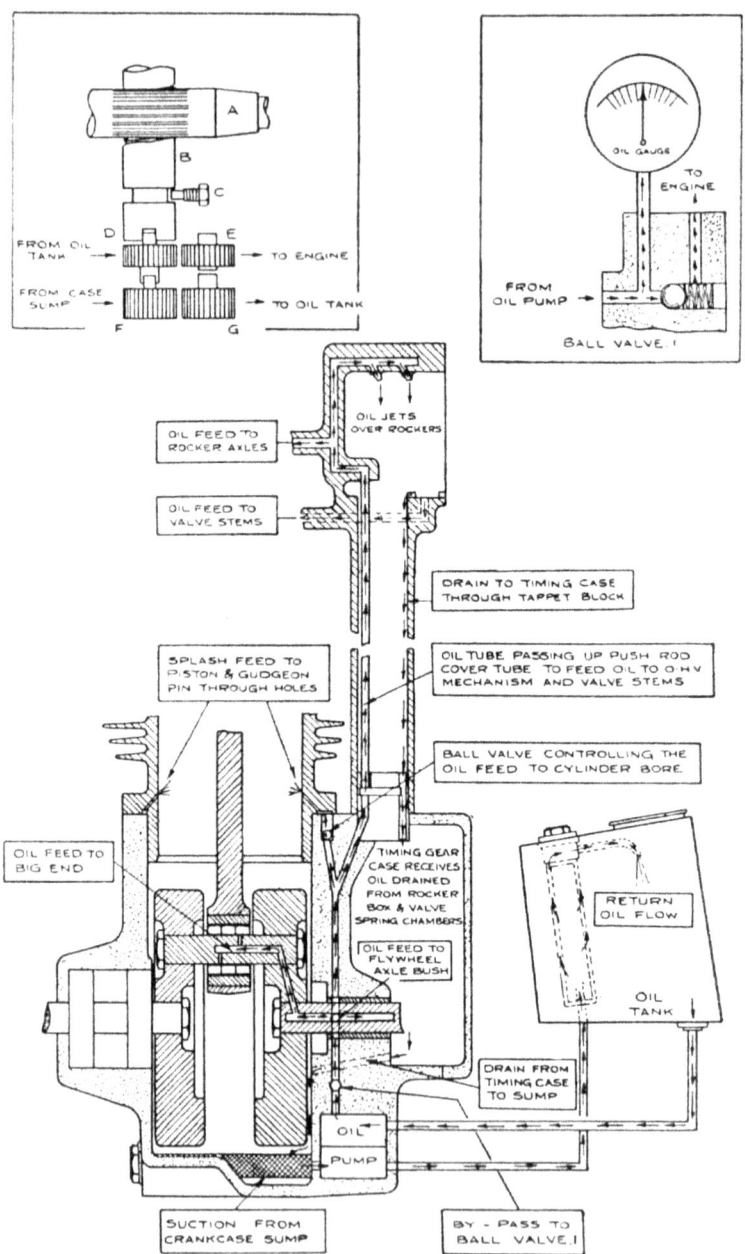

Fig. 10. Details of 1939 Dry-sump Lubrication System
This applies to all the O.H.V. "high-camshaft" engines

LUBRICATION

at the same time. The first of these will be found by unscrewing the supply pipe and regulator. To remove the second one, detach the short suction sump to pump pipe, when the filter can be removed by unscrewing the large hexagon nut at the base of the sump. When any of the oil pipes are detached, they must be replaced so that all air leaks are avoided, and it is essential that the pipes are re-connected correctly. Otherwise, the whole circulatory system will be put out of order.

The Model 10, first introduced in 1931, has the oil in the sump, although the dry sump system is employed. There is a large hexagon shaped filler at the front of the sump for the purpose of filling and the sump holds one quart of oil. The oil flow is regulated by a knurled knob at the side of the timing cover, and the position for all normal running is about one full turn from the fully closed position. The tell-tale on this machine is situated at the side of the regulator. To clean the filter on this model unscrew the large nut below the regulator.

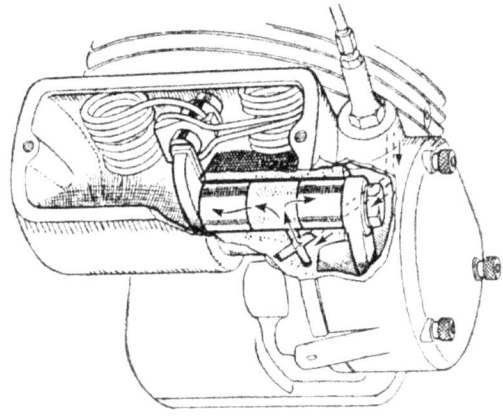

FIG. 11. SHOWING OVERHEAD ROCKER LUBRICATION
(*From "The Motor Cycle"*)

Dry-sump Lubrication (1939 O.H.V.). Although the dry-sump system formerly used is still employed, there is a slight difference. Reference to Fig. 10 shows that the oil-pump drive is obtained by a spiral cut on the outer end of the timing-side flywheel shaft A. Engaging with a similar gear cut on the upper end of the vertical shaft B is a guide screw used to locate the shaft. The oil-pump gears D and E driven by the vertical shaft are a close fit in the oil-pump housing, and the rotary movement of the gears forces the oil out into the desired channels.

The oil circulation will be easily followed by observance of the diagram. Oil passes first through the ball valve and then through an oil-way to the timing-side crankshaft bush and ball bearing. A feed is provided through the centre of the timing-side flywheel and on to the big-end, any surplus being thrown out on to the cylinder walls. The piston, gudgeon pin, and bush have an additional feed via a channel cut in the lower part of the cylinder barrel. A pipe leading up inside the push-rod cover tube provides a copious supply of oil for the rockers (Fig. 11), rocker bushes, and push-rod ends. The surplus is used to lubricate the valve guides and tappets, and by allowing the oil to build up to a predetermined level a continuous supply is provided for the timing chain.

Oil Feed to Inlet-valve Guide (1939 O.H.V.). The needle-valve screw for the oil feed to the inlet-valve guide is set at the works, and should not be altered unless absolutely necessary. The approximate correct setting is *half a turn* open from the fully closed position. Adjustment to the valve may be necessary if the plug oils up or an excessive amount of smoke is seen escaping from the exhaust pipe. To eradicate these defects, screw the adjuster into the head a trifle at a time. If it is necessary to increase the flow on account of the inlet valve squeaking, unscrew the valve slightly, bearing in mind that a slight movement of the screw makes a considerable difference to the flow of oil.

CHAPTER III

THE ENGINE

IT is reasonable to suppose that almost everyone interested in motor-cycling has an elementary knowledge of the working of the various components, but for the benefit of the novice it is proposed to give an outline of the general principles of the engine.

How It Works. Motor-cycle engines consist of two types. The first is called the two-stroke and the second the four-stroke or the "Otto" cycle. As all Sunbeam engines are of the four-stroke type, the principles which govern the two-stroke will be ignored, and that of the four-stroke is given herewith. The principle on which all internal combustion engines work is quite straightforward, inasmuch as the energy produced by the expansion of gases after heating is employed. In the motor-cycle engine, the gases are trapped and made to expand at one end of the cylinder in which a piston is made a gas-tight fit, but which is free to move up and down. The piston is connected by a crank, the connecting rod to the fly-wheels, so that when the explosion occurs and the piston is thrust downwards, the downward movement is converted to a rotary one. The rotation of the fly-wheels provides the driving motion for the rear wheel, although there are various stages in between. This is the simplest exposition of how the "wheels go round," but obviously many other factors must be taken into consideration. Clearly, both the gas which is exploded in the cylinder and the means by which it is fired must be provided, and the two devices which attend to this part of the business are known respectively as the carburettor and magneto. The carburettor is the instrument which provides the explosive matter by mixing air and petrol in certain prescribed proportions. The magneto attends to the firing part of the business. Obviously, it is imperative that these operations be conducted in their proper order, and for this purpose other mechanism must be introduced. This mechanism, which works in conjunction with the piston, is known as the valves, and the attendant drive for these is known as the timing gear. These two valves, one inlet and the other exhaust, allow the fresh gas from the carburettor to be sucked in on the downward piston stroke and expelled when burnt on the upward piston stroke, *via* the exhaust valve. In order that the valves should perform their allotted tasks in the correct order timing cams are fitted inside the crankcase. These timing cams lift the valve every alternate revolution by means of a pinion which drives from the engine mainshaft. Owing to the small diameter of the valve stem, there would be a "hammering effect" at the point of contact between the valve stem and the cams, and to overcome this a rocker or cam lever is interposed between the two.

THE FOUR-STROKE CYCLE

The explosive gas has to be drawn into the cylinder, compressed, fired, and then passed out by means of the exhaust port.

Inlet. The inlet valve opens and the piston descends. A partial vacuum is formed and this produces a suction from the carburettor *via* the induction pipe. The blast of air sweeps over the carburettor jet, through which there is a constant supply of petrol, and causes a fine jet of petrol similar to a fountain. This fountain forms itself into a spray and the resultant mixture passes along the induction pipe into the cylinder in its most easily combustible form. As the piston reaches the end of its downward stroke, the inlet valve closes and, as nothing else at the top opens, the cylinder becomes a sealed chamber containing the mixture ready for explosion.

Compression. The piston, having reached the bottom of its stroke, commences to rise again and, due to the presence of the piston rings, the gas is unable to escape down the sides and therefore the charge in the cylinder is compressed into a much smaller space than it previously occupied. This space varies according to the design of the engine.

Combustion. The stage is now all set for the charge to be fired, and this is brought about by a spark appearing at the sparking plug points and igniting the gases. This spark, which is supplied by the magneto, does not, however, occur just as the piston reaches what is known as "Top Dead Centre" (T.D.C.). The correct timing of the spark is dependent upon the speed at which the engine is running. The reason for this is that the explosion of a mixture of air and petrol vapour takes an appreciable time, causing a lag between the passage of the spark and the time when the exploded gases reach their maximum temperature and pressure. If, therefore, the engine is running at a fast speed, the ignition or spark must be timed to take place early to enable the maximum pressure to take place when the piston has just passed top dead point. Should the spark occur too early, what is known as "knocking" or "pinking" will ensue. This phenomenon is generally attributed to the fact that the early spark ignites some portion of the gas before the whole is compressed and a blow is administered to the top of the piston. On the other hand, if the spark should

THE ENGINE

occur too late the piston will have moved some distance on its downward stroke, and consequently some of the energy of the explosion will be lost. Actually, the combustion stroke is the

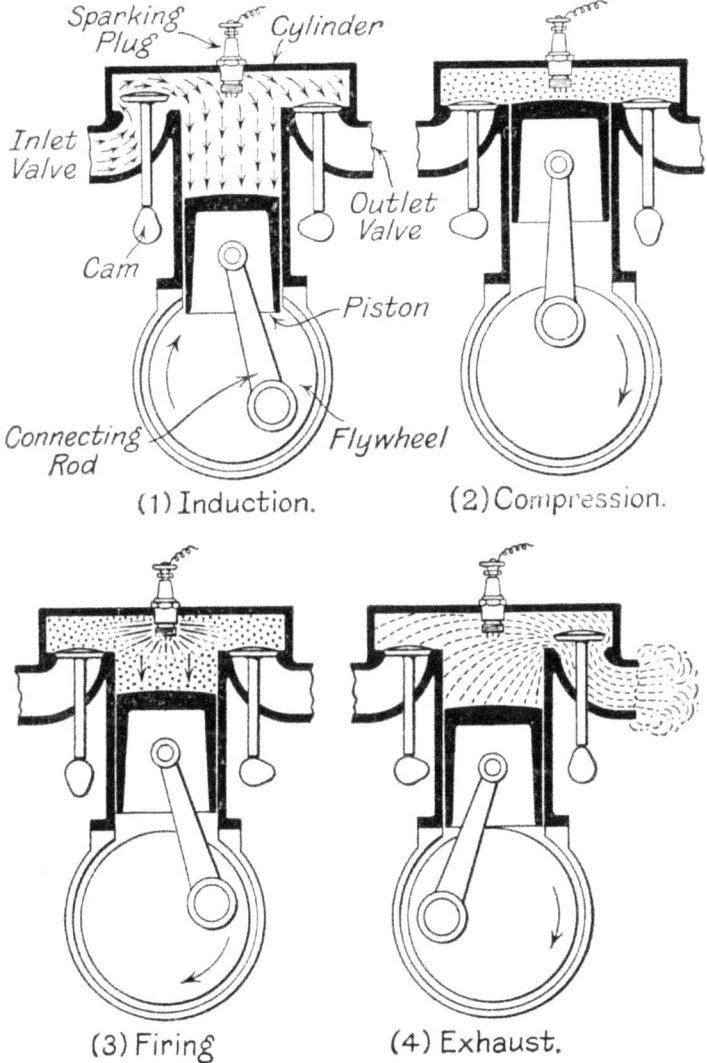

Fig. 12. The Principle of the Four-stroke Engine

only power impulse of the four-stroke inasmuch as it is this stroke which drives the piston down.

Exhaust Stroke. To complete the cycle, the exhaust valve now opens and the exhaust gases are expelled from the cylinder by the ascending piston. After being cooled by allowing them to expand in the silencers, the gases finally escape into the atmosphere at approximately the top of the stroke. When the exhaust valve closes the inlet valve reopens and the cycle of operations is repeated.

The above is a brief exposition of the *modus operandi* of the internal combustion engine as applied to the motor-cycle. The two components referred to rather briefly—the magneto and carburettor—will be dealt with fully later on.

DECARBONIZING

As even the best of machines will not run for ever and a certain amount of wear must inevitably take place, it is proposed to deal next with all the adjustments and overhauls necessary to keep the machine in first-class order. This information it is hoped will be of assistance both to the novice and to the expert rider. In every internal combustion engine, what is known as carbon forms a deposit on the internal parts after a fairly lengthy period (approximately 2,000 miles) has been covered, and this must be removed. This deposit is inevitable and is due to three things : (*a*) Carbonization of road dust, which is generally sucked into the engine *via* the air intake. (*b*) Incomplete fuel combustion. (*c*) Lubricating oil working its way into the combustion chamber and being burnt in the process. Carbon is very detrimental to the running of the engine, and makes its presence felt in several disagreeable forms. The engine loses its original "pep" and there is a definite decline in the general performance. This is accompanied by a "woolly" or muffled exhaust note and a tendency for the engine to knock under the slightest provocation. If by retarding the ignition lever considerably the "knocking" disappears, it is a sure sign that the time has come for the engine to be decarbonized and the valves ground-in. It is always advisable to remove the valves when carrying out a top overhaul, as not only does this facilitate the cleaning out of the parts, but also enables one to examine the valves and seats for any signs of pitting. Although, actually speaking, the general process of decarbonizing is the same, owing to the different designs, i.e. side valve and overhead valve engines, the operations will be described separately.

Side Valve Engine. Probably the engine which has found its way into the hands of the largest section of the general riding public is that depicted in Fig. 13, the famous Longstroke, so called because of its 102 mm. stroke, and it is proposed to deal with this first. It should be borne in mind that the present day Lion model has a detachable head, and this is dealt with in a similar fashion to the O.H.V. models described later.

THE ENGINE

First Operation. Before tackling the dismantling of the various components it is as well to check up the tools and the various functions for which they are intended. All the machines are equipped with a screwdriver, pliers, oil squirt, grease-gun, tyre pump, and the following spanners.

Fig. 13. Longstroke Engine with Valve Chamber Cover Removed

(A) T.1. Double-ended open spanner which fits all the $\frac{1}{4}$ in. and $\frac{5}{16}$ in. nuts.

T.1A. Double-ended spanner which fits all the nuts $\frac{1}{8}$ in. and $\frac{3}{16}$ in.

T.2. Double-ended bent spanner, fits the hub cone lock-nuts and magneto holding-down nuts.

T.3. Double-ended ring spanner, fits all nuts $\frac{7}{16}$ in. and $\frac{1}{2}$ in.

T.4. Double-ended ring spanner, fits all nuts $\frac{5}{16}$ in. and $\frac{3}{8}$ in.

T.5. Adjustable spanner.

T.6. Tappet adjusting spanner.

T.7. Spanner for exhaust union (M. 10).

T.8. Spanner for exhaust union (M. 9 and Lion).

T.9. Spanner for finned exhaust union (M. 90 only).

T.10. Pair of spanners for adjusting the cones (interchangeable wheels).

T.11. Tubular spanner for the three pins securing the wheel to the hub.

T.12. Open-ended flat spanner to fit ¾ in. nuts on rear brake.

T.13. Tubular spanner for main clutch nut.

T.14. Spanner for gear-box sprocket lock-nut and head lock-nut.

T.15. Valve spring clamp for hairpin valve springs fitted to Model 90.

T.19. Tubular spanner for cylinder head screws (Lion models).

The two following tools are supplied by the works and these will be found to be extremely useful when decarbonizing.

T.16. The O.H.V. valve grinding tool. This tool grips round the valve stem and enables the valve to be pulled up hard against its seat and easily turned, thus greatly facilitating the grinding-in process.

T.16. Valve spring compressor for O.H.V. coil springs. It is advisable to use a lever of some sort in conjunction with this tool, as the springs are very strong. A long piece of wood makes an excellent lever.

When using the above tools, remember that a good mechanic only uses the spanner which *fits* the nuts; for example, do not use the ¾ in. brakes spanner, T.12, on the hub spindle nuts. The right spanner is the double-ended ring T.3.

Remember the old saying, "Cleanliness is next to Godliness," and see that the garage is perfectly clean. Have several boxes handy to place the various parts in as they are removed and a tin of paraffin. The engine should be thoroughly cleaned with paraffin before the dismantling process is commenced, as any dirt or grit which is left about may work into the bearings and cause any amount of trouble. Next, remove all the components which obstruct the easy removal of the cylinder.

Removing Carburettor. The first item to tackle is the carburettor. Undo petrol pipe union nut at bottom of float chamber. Unscrew the knurled cap at the top of carburettor, thus enabling the throttle and air slides to be removed. If the screw holding the clip to the induction pipe be loosened the carburettor may be removed.

With the carburettor safely removed, the following parts may then be taken off. The exhaust pipe may be disconnected by unscrewing the union nut, followed by unscrewing the valve caps. A special spanner is provided for the last two items and it is advisable to use this, as sometimes they may be found to be a little obstreperous. The wisest policy is to slacken them a trifle

THE ENGINE

while the engine is still warm, but in any case never use excessive brute force, as there is a possibility that the threads will either strip or the cylinder distort. A valve cap which has resisted all efforts to remove it may sometimes be shifted by a liberal dose of paraffin oil and leaving it overnight.

Removing Cylinder. Engage top gear and turn rear wheel backwards until the piston is at its lowest point (Bottom Dead Centre). After removing the four cylinder holding-down nuts at the base, carefully raise the cylinder and turn it halfway round so that the induction pipe is pointing forwards. Be careful not to put any strain on the connecting rod and lift the cylinder perfectly square. When the top piston ring can be seen emerging from the barrel, be careful to prevent the piston from swinging away on the connecting rod and striking the crankcase, as this may cause it to distort or perhaps fracture. Should the barrel stick a little at first, a sharp blow with the closed hand on each side will usually cause it to free itself.

As soon as the cylinder is withdrawn, a cloth should be laid over the opening for the connecting rod, so that any foreign matter, such as particles of carbon, cannot fall into the crankcase.

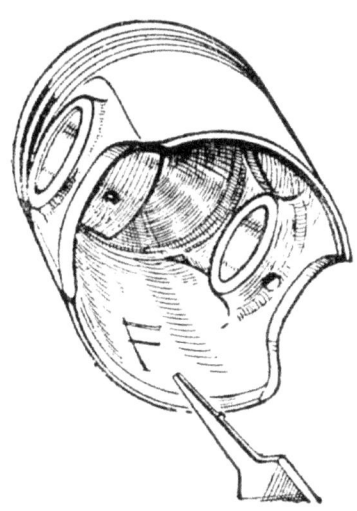

FIG. 14. MARKING INSIDE OF PISTON TO ENSURE CORRECT REPLACEMENT
(*From "The Motor-Cycle"*)

In the case of some longstroke engines, and also the $4\frac{1}{4}$ h.p. Model 7, when the sidecar clip is in position on the front down tube there is very little clearance, and on these machines it is necessary to withdraw the gudgeon pin and slip the piston up into the cylinder. If this is done there will be ample clearance.

Piston Removal. Almost all Sunbeams have a "floating" gudgeon pin and it is a comparatively simple matter to remove this. Where spring circlips are fitted, they must first be removed by pinching their free end together with a small pair of pliers when the gudgeon pin may be pushed out from either end. On machines with fixed gudgeon pins, the latter must be withdrawn from the piston through the hole marked "IN," i.e. the split pin must be removed from the "OTHER" end. Replace similarly through the hole marked "IN." If the gudgeon pin has an oil groove see that it is replaced with the groove on *top*. The earlier type aluminium pistons are not marked "IN," but the gudgeon pin can only be removed and replaced in the correct direction as it has only one split pin, a permanent pin being fixed at the other end. As the piston will have, to a certain degree, worn a path or a slight groove in the cylinder barrel, it is advisable to mark it in the manner indicated in Fig. 14. This ensures that the piston is fitted the correct way round when the engine is re-assembled.

Piston Rings. It is advisable to remove the piston rings in order to clean out the ring groove and also to test their elasticity.

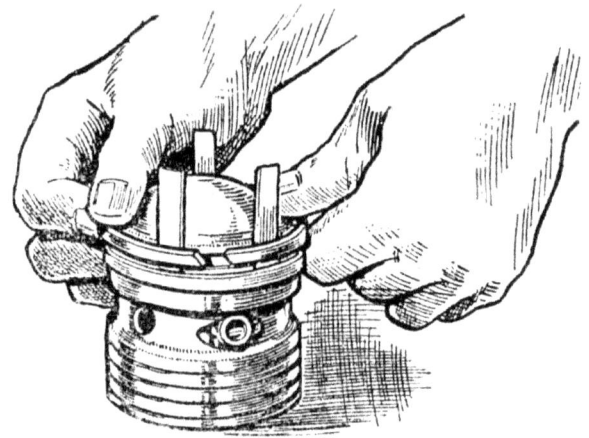

FIG. 15. REMOVING PISTON RINGS

The piston rings have the onerous duty of seeing that the gases do not escape when under compression, and they therefore fulfil a very important function. The rings are made of cast iron and exceedingly brittle, and so it behoves the rider to treat them very gently, otherwise they will snap very easily. As they cannot be opened wider than will allow them to slip over the piston crown, the best plan is to insert three slips of tin about $\frac{1}{4}$ in. wide and to work them round the back of the ring until equally placed. Fig. 15 will indicate what is required. The rings will then be free to slip off quite easily without damage. The condition of the rings is important and the following will assist in determining whether they should be replaced or not. If they are found to have plenty of tension, are free in the grooves and bright all the way round, then it will be quite satisfactory to replace them. If, on the other hand, they are dull at some points, thus proving that they are not in proper contact with the cylinder walls or have no "spring" in them, they should be renewed. Similarly, if they are

THE ENGINE

vertically loose in the grooves they should be replaced. Rings sometimes stick in their grooves through burnt oil and they can generally be loosened with paraffin. If the grooves are then cleaned out properly and the rings replaced, they will probably function correctly. Whenever a cylinder is re-bored, it is advisable to ascertain what the oversize bore is, in order that the correct oversize piston rings are obtained when these are renewed. The 1929 and later engines have scraper piston rings fitted, and the correct way to replace these is with the wider part uppermost. When replacing the rings, take care that the gaps are not all in line, and when the cylinder is being refitted see that the rings are not broken by being forced out of their grooves. When fitting new rings they should be inserted in the cylinder barrel at a point in the piston travel and tested for clearance. The reason for this is to allow for expansion as incorrectly-fitted rings might possibly overlap and then break. The correct ring gap on the longstroke is 0·010 in. for the top ring, 0·008 in. for the second, and 0·006 in. for the bottom. These clearances will be found eminently satisfactory for ordinary road work but may be increased a little all round if high speeds are indulged in. In case of doubt it is recommended that only piston rings supplied by the manufacturers should be used.

Removing Carbon. To remove the carbon from a longstroke cylinder barrel, use a long screwdriver and chip the deposit from the head and the exhaust port. The piston should be cleaned with an old penknife and finished off with fine emery paper. As aluminium is very soft, be careful not to dig the knife in too deeply. The piston crown may be given a final clean with metal polish.

The object of giving the piston top a very clean surface is to prevent the accumulation of carbon. Make no attempt to remove the carbon from the piston skirt. It is highly injurious to clean piston sides with emery cloth or anything of a similar nature as this will act as an abrasive and cause rapid wear of both the cylinder bore and piston. The other parts where carbon may be found are on the inside of the piston and the ring grooves. The back of the rings should be scraped, cleaned, and then washed in paraffin before replacement.

Removing Overhead Valve Cylinder Head. As the process of decarbonizing the cylinder head of the O.H.V. model is similar to that of S.V., it is proposed to deal only with the dismantling of the O.H.V. head. Although it is possible to remove the cylinder without disturbing anything else, accessibility is greatly improved by removing the tank, although this necessitates the saddle being removed. First, then, detach the petrol pipe at the tap end, making sure that the tap has been turned off. Remove the gear-operating rod from the change speed lever by undoing bolt and nut as in Fig. 16. Note that this should be replaced with the washer between the change speed lever and the operating rod and not behind the nut. Spring the loops holding the Bowden cables open just enough for the cables to be released. Remove the saddle by loosening the two nuts which hold the clamp to the seat pin. If the four nuts underneath the tank, together with their attendant lock-nuts, are removed, the tank may be lifted off. The machines previous to the saddle tank models have bolts which screw into the tank but these are removed in the same way. Next remove the sparking plug, carburettor and exhaust pipe or pipes, as described for the S.V. models. Slacken the locking nuts at the base of the two push-rod tubes, shown in Fig. 17, and screw these down until they are clear of the rocker-box above.

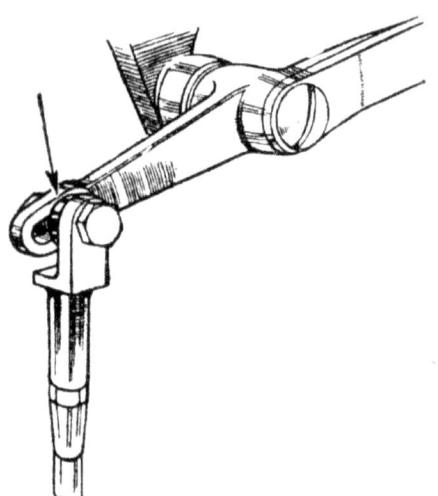

FIG. 16. THE WASHER ON THE GEAR-ROD SHACKLE NUT MUST BE BETWEEN THE LEVER AND THE SHACKLE

(*From "The Motor-Cycle"*)

On the 1929-31 machines, the rocker-box, shown in Fig. 18, is held in place by four $\frac{5}{16}$ pins screwed to the cylinder head, two for each side plate. If these are removed, the rocker-box will come away complete. The earlier O.H.V. models simply have a rocker-plate each side secured in a similar manner, the rocker-gear not being enclosed. If the four long sleeve nuts, shown in Fig. 19, which hold the cylinder head to the barrel are undone, the head may be removed. Some of these sleeve nuts are fitted with slots which enable them to be loosened very quickly with the aid of a screwdriver, once a spanner has been used on the initial threads. In the case of an O.H.V. engine, if only a top overhaul is being carried out and there is plenty of compression, the cylinder barrel need not be disturbed. The piston top may be cleaned *in situ*, and after the head has been decoked, it may be replaced. If, however, it is desired to remove the piston, the cylinder barrel can be lifted up and away from the four long holding-down studs which are screwed into the crankcase. For 1937-9, see pages 117-123.

THE ENGINE

Grinding-in Valves. As it is essential that the valves and valve seats should be gas-tight, it is advisable to examine these periodically. If they are found to show signs of pitting (i.e. very small holes appear on the surfaces), the valves should be ground-in.

Removing Valves (S.V.). The best method to remove the valves is to employ a Terry valve spring compressor, obtainable from

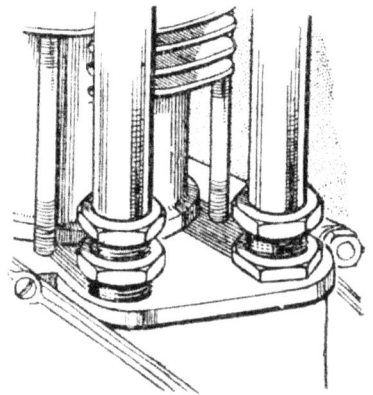

FIG. 17. WHEN THE PUSH-ROD COVER NUTS HAVE BEEN SLACKENED THE COVERS MUST BE SCREWED DOWN (PRE-1939)
(*From "The Motor-Cycle"*)

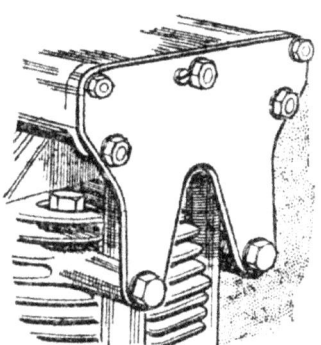

FIG. 18. THE SIDE-PLATE OF 1929–31 ROCKER-BOX
(*From "The Motor-Cycle"*)

most accessory dealers. Insert the hooked end of the valve compressor into the cylinder so that it bears on the valve head. By placing the forked end under the spring and levering upwards, the valve cotter may be withdrawn with the aid of a pair of pliers. The valve cotters are oblong pieces of steel which fit into a slot in the valve stem. With the removal of the cotter the valve spring will drop down and the valve may be pushed up through the cylinder and removed.

Removing Valves (O.H.V. Hairpin). As there are two types of valve springs employed in the O.H.V. Sunbeams, they will be dealt with separately. The hairpin type valve springs, which are almost a unique feature of the Model 90, have several advantages, amongst which are: enormous strength, and, owing to their length, the engine heat does not affect them greatly, thus enabling the "temper" of the spring to be maintained over a lengthy period. This type of spring may be removed by a special clamp provided by the makers, Fig. 20. This clamp is simply pushed over the spring and the bolt at the top, and screwed down. When the spring in compressed sufficiently it may be withdrawn. When both the inner and outer springs have been removed, the valve will drop down.

Removing Valves (O.H.V. Coil). To remove the overhead valves fitted with coil springs, place a wood block in the cylinder head to prevent the valve opening and, with the special valve spring compressor provided by the makers (Fig. 20), press down heavily on

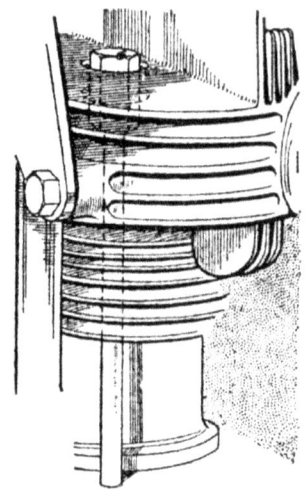

Fig. 19. The Cylinder Head is Retained by Long Sleeve Nuts, for which a Box Spanner must be Used (1930)

(*From "The Motor-Cycle"*)

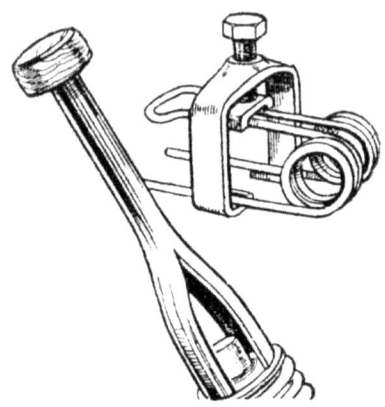

Fig. 20. Two Special Tools for Compressing—(below) Coil and (above) Hair-pin Valve Springs

(*From "The Motor-Cycle"*)

the valve spring cup. When the spring is depressed enough, pick out the split collars by means of a thin screwdriver. These collars clamp round the valve stem, and when they are removed the valve springs will relax their tension and enable the valve to be released. The valve should be ground-in with carborundum paste, to which, when the actual grinding process is being carried out, a little oil may be added.

The valve heads on the side valve models have slots in them in order that a screwdriver may be used. When the valve has been treated with a small quantity of grinding paste and a little oil, it should be pressed down hard on the seating and turned backwards and forwards. To prevent the valve being ground in the one place, occasionally lift it from its seat and give it a twist, allowing it to drop back in a different position.

Owing to the design, the overhead valves are pulled up against their seating, not pressed down as in the case of the S.V., and for this purpose a special tool is provided by the makers to grip the end of the valve stem. It will be found, generally, that the tins which are sold containing grinding paste are labelled "Fine" and "Coarse." Only use the "Fine" unless the seatings are deeply pitted, when in the latter case it is permissible to commence the operations with a little "Coarse." The valve head and stem should be cleaned, and for this purpose a bench drill will be found very useful. Grip the valve in the chuck and rotate the valve, polishing it with fine emery cloth and finally finishing off with metal polish. Take care that the ends of the valve stems are not burred, otherwise undue wear of the tappet pins will take place. When all the pit marks have been removed and the valves nicely polished, they should be washed in paraffin to remove all traces of emery or grinding powder. As may be readily understood, anything of such a highly abrasive nature as the above will cause excessive wear. The cylinder head itself should be carefully cleaned out and polished with metal polish. When the parts have all been washed in paraffin and dried with a soft, dry rag, they are ready to be re-assembled.

Re-assembling. Re-assembling the various parts after a "decoke" is largely a matter of putting everything back as it was previously. The main points to remember are: When refitting the valves, smear graphite on the stems to prevent them binding in guides. Oil the gudgeon pin before replacing it in the connecting rod. Smear the piston thoroughly with oil, especially by the rings, and wipe off the excess which sometimes works on to the piston crown. The top of the crankcase and the base of the cylinder should be perfectly clean and even, and if the paper washer is at all crumpled or broken, it should be replaced. Smear both sides of the washer with gold size or one of the well-known jointing compounds. In the case of the O.H.V. models, the cylinder head fits on the barrel by a plain joint. To prevent any oil or compression leakage, this should be ground-in, in a similar way to that of the valves. It will be found much simpler to grind the head into the barrel if the operation is carried out when the barrel is removed from the machine. *On no account attempt to use a washer at this point.* The valve cap copper asbestos washers should be renewed if they show signs of warping or leaking. When replacing the rocker-box on the 1929-31 O.H.V. models, do not forget the spring washers on the four screws which hold the rocker-plates to the cylinder head, and do not screw the push-rod tubes too tightly up against the rocker-box. The cylinder holding-down sleeve nuts should be screwed down evenly. If the nuts are screwed down tightly one at a time there will be a tendency to distort the cylinder head. When the re-assembling process is completed the engine should be started and very gently warmed up. Go over all the nuts, especially the cylinder holding-down nuts, and then check the tappet adjustment.

Rocker-box and Overhead Valve Gear. The rocker-boxes on the 1932 models, illustrated in Fig. 21, are very ingeniously con-

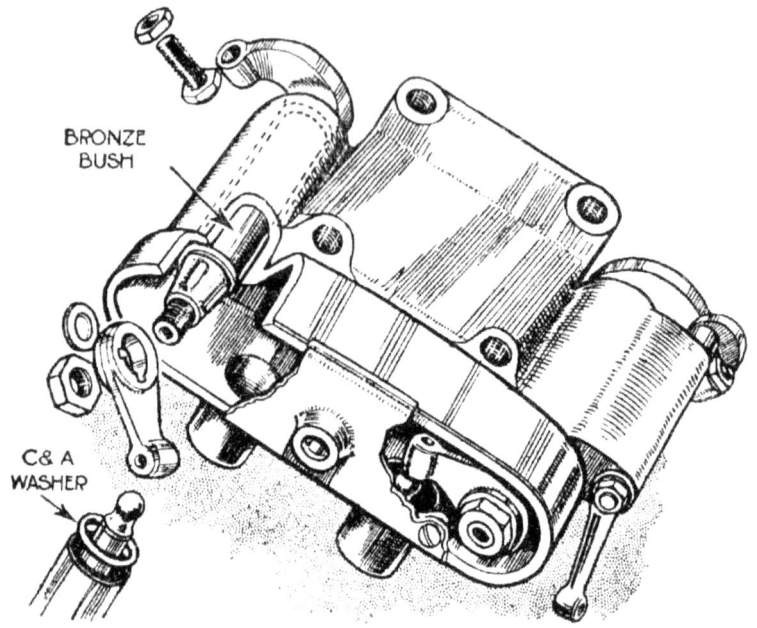

Fig. 21. An "Exploded" View of the 1932 Rocker-box
(*From "The Motor-Cycle"*)

structed, and it is inadvisable to tamper with them, and, owing to the fact that oil is pumped under pressure to the rocker-shafts, push-rod ends and valve guides, no attention should be required at this point for a considerable period. The following remarks apply to the type of rocker-gear employed from 1929 to 1931.

Rocker-box and Rockers, 1929-31. If the rocker-box is suspected as being the cause of any exceptional valve gear noise, it can be examined for wear. There should be no up-and-down play of the rockers on their spindles, and very slight movement sideways. If the former is considerable, it is advisable to dismantle the box. First detach the two side plates; this will expose the complete mechanism of the box to view. On the right-hand side of the box will be seen the rocker-arms. Unscrew the ¾ in. nuts and remove the spring washers. Give the ends of the rocker-shafts a sharp blow with a lead punch and hammer, and the rocker-arms will come away, as they are only keyed to the rocker-shafts. The latter can then be withdrawn from the bushes. It is unlikely that the wear, if any, will be due to a worn shaft, and in most cases it is the phosphor-bronze bushes that are found to be at fault. These are a press fit and are easily renewable.

If the rocker-box is of the early 1929 type, it is wise on re-assembling it to fit two light spring washers behind the rocker-arms; these will cut out practically all rattle due to excessive lateral movement. These washers are fitted as standard to the 1930 and 1931 rocker-boxes.

Care should be taken, if new bushes and spring washers have been fitted, that, on tightening up the rocker-arm locking-nuts, the shafts do not bind up solid. If this happens—as it frequently does—then it is necessary to face down the bush and the aluminium casing about $\frac{1}{16}$ in. until the right amount of lateral movement is obtained—which is three to four thous. This task is best entrusted to experienced hands; besides being a fiddling job—as the box has to be continually dismantled and re-erected—it has also to be carried out with great care in order to ensure the casing is cut away evenly; otherwise, trouble will certainly follow.

A further addition to later models, and one that is worth fitting to boxes without it, is a cranked grease nipple, Fig. 22, for each rocker-spindle. The case is drilled and tapped just by the flat portion behind the rockers themselves;

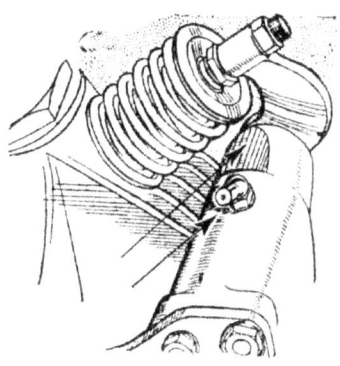

Fig. 22. On the Rocker-boxes of the Later Models there are Cranked Grease Gun Nipples

These can be conveniently fitted to earlier models by drilling and tapping the flat section indicated

(*From "The Motor-Cycle"*)

that is, on the right-hand side. This ensures a constant supply of grease to pack the bearings, and it is surprising how any tendency of the gear to rattle is lessened by this means. The nipples should be lubricated every 300 or 400 miles. The 1931 boxes are fitted with steel bushes and hollow rocker-shafts with nipples screwed into their ends. The owners of 1931 models will have to make frequent use of the above-mentioned nipples in order to avoid the possibility of a rocker seizing, as steel in this case is bearing against steel.

The cups set in the ends of the rocker-arms, and the ball ends of the push-rods which engage in them, should also be examined, specially if it has been found that continual tappet adjustment has been necessary. The cups are press-in fits and can be punched out by way of the hole drilled through the top of the rocker-arm just above the cup. The ball ends of the push-rods are also renewable and are sweated into the push-rod. To detach them, heat the end of the push-rod and give the ball a sharp twist and pull with pliers. Clean the interior of the push-rod; tin the body of the new ball end, and, while it is hot, press it into the push-rod.

When the rocker-box is re-assembled, care must be taken to see that the joints are absolutely clean and that a smear of gold size is employed in order to ensure that there are no oil or air leaks.

DISMANTLING ENGINE

Assuming that the rider will have carried out quite a number of "decokes" before any further overhauls are necessary, it is proposed to deal with the further dismantling of the engine only after it has been prepared for decarbonizing.

Testing for Big End Wear. After the machine has covered a considerable mileage, a certain amount of play may be found to exist in the big end, and to ascertain this, bring the connecting rod to top dead centre and endeavour to move it up and down vertically. If there should be any movement whatsoever, the big end assembly should be replaced. A certain amount of side play may also be noticed, but unless excessive this may be ignored. Practically speaking, the only time the engine need be stripped, further than for decarbonizing, is when the renewal of the big end becomes due. To remove the fly-wheels, proceed as under.

Remove footrest assembly complete by undoing the nuts of the end of the rod and driving the rod through from either side. Remove the oil pipes, the supply from tank to pump, and the return from pump to tank, also the oil gauge pipes on the 1932 machines. Remove the exhaust valve lifter wire by compressing the volute spring with a screwdriver and pulling out the inner wire with a pair of pliers. Remove the magneto chain cover by unscrewing the seven screws on the outside. The oil pump will come away complete with the chain cover. Should the removal of the magneto or "Magdyno" be required, it will be necessary to procure the spindle extractor provided by the manufacturers. The long sleeve nut in the magneto shaft should be unscrewed and the extractor screwed on until the magneto sprocket is forced off. The chain can be lifted off with the sprocket. Unscrew the ten screws holding the timing cover to the crankcase. The cover can then be lifted off, exposing the timing gear.

So far we have only dealt with the timing side. The driving side, i.e. chain cases, etc., is dealt with elsewhere. Undo the twelve nuts on the engine bolts, and the latter which pass through the

THE ENGINE

engine plates may be knocked out. Get someone to take the weight of the unit as the last bolt is being removed.

The crankcase unit is now quite free and may be lowered to the ground. An extra pair of hands is an enormous asset at this point, as the unit will be found fairly heavy, and it must on no account be allowed to drop heavily on the ground. The crankcase should be removed to a bench to facilitate working on it.

Before dividing the crankcase, it will be as well to check wear in the mainshaft bearings and the amount of end float in the shafts.

To make a good job, there should be no up-and-down play at either end of the shaft after the bearings have been washed out with paraffin. If there is any appreciable amount of movement, the bearings must be renewed.

After undoing the twelve $\frac{1}{4}$ in. nuts on the studs which pass through the crankcase, there is nothing to prevent the latter being parted. Request someone to hold the crankcase a few inches off the bench, gripping only the driving side half with the drive side mainshaft uppermost. A sharp blow on the end of the shaft with a copper or lead hammer will invariably part the two halves.

The Fly-wheel Assembly. The connecting rod, big end, and fly-wheels play an extremely important part in the running of a machine, and it is absolutely essential that they run in perfect harmony. Badly balanced fly-wheels are of incalculable harm and will result in the machine vibrating excessively, and also cause enormous overloading of the mainshaft bearings. It is for these reasons the author would recommend that when a big end replacement becomes necessary, it is advisable to send the fly-wheel assembly either to the works or one of the service depots. However, for those competent enough to undertake the parting of the fly-wheels, the following will be of assistance.

Big End Renewal. On removing the fly-wheels, shown in Fig. 23, the roller bearing centres should draw off the shafts without much difficulty. (Bearing in mind that all engines with an extension to the mainshaft beyond the centre pinion must have a left-hand thread and a parallel keyed centre pinion. All other engines have a right-hand thread and a tapered keyed pinion.)

If the bearing centres are immovable, a good plan is to drop the outside bearing ring about two-thirds over the rollers and lever it up with two tyre levers from the bottom of the rollers, and, when it has moved about $\frac{1}{8}$ in., the leverage may be shifted to the solid portion of the bearing. If the outside bearing ring is omitted, the rollers will be forced from their housing and the bearing will become useless. Next remove the crankpin nuts. Stand the flywheels upon the bench, steady with the left hand, and strike the crankpin a heavy blow with a copper hammer. This method will remove the tightest crankpin. Before proceeding further, the truth of the individual shafts must be verified and trued up if necessary, noting beforehand that the centres in the shafts are undamaged. The crankpin may now be fitted, but should the tapered ends of the crankpin have very sharp edges, these must

FIG. 23. THE FLYWHEELS AND TIMING PINION (MODEL 9)

be ground off, otherwise the crankpin will probably cut into the wheel and ruin it. To be a good fit, the crankpin should push in about two-thirds of the way by hand. If the crankpin has one side fitted with a key, that side must be fitted first, but it must be remembered that the second wheel can only be drawn on the pin by the nut. Therefore it is best to drive the plain tapers right home on the wheels with a copper hammer. Remove it and drive the keyed side right home and bolt it up finally. If it is found impossible to drive the pin right home, the hole may be enlarged by very carefully scraping, but this should be done only in extreme circumstances, as it is very easy to spoil a good wheel. We now come to the connecting rod bushes or big end and small end bushes as they are most frequently known. With ordinary care, these may be fitted with the help of a large vice, using a piece of tubing or something similar, slightly smaller in diameter than the outside of the bush, and another piece slightly larger on the inside than the outside of the bush.

From the above the method of removing and refitting the bushes will be obvious. Of course, if the rider has access to a press or to

FIG. 24. BIG END ASSEMBLY, CONNECTING ROD, CRANKPIN, ROLLER CAGE, WASHERS, AND $\frac{5}{16}$ IN. ROLLERS

proper bush removing tools, the job will be much easier. As the bushes distort and contract when fitted, they must be ground or renewed as the case may be. The small end bush must be reamered out with an adjustable reamer, remembering not to turn the reamer backwards as this blunts the edges. A gudgeon pin is correctly fitted when it is dead free without any side shake. The oil hole and groove must be put in *after* the bush is fitted.

To fit the big end bush to the rollers and crankpin it is best to fix the fly-wheels in the vice by the mainshaft (with clamps) so that the crankpin is up straight. Assemble the washer, cage and rollers, shown in Fig. 24, on the crankpin, making sure that the cage is sound and in good condition. The big end bush may then be externally ground to fit. Although it is very nice to fit a connecting rod to have no side shake, it *must* be borne in mind that the slightest bending or stiffness in a roller bearing may cause the bearing surface to skin and eventually break up. When a satisfactory fit has been obtained the other washer and wheel may then be fitted. As the last end of the crankpin has already been driven right home in the wheel, it is a matter of certainty that the second nut will be able to draw the second wheel right home. Tighten the nut as far as possible, holding the wheels by hand, previously having lined up the wheels with a straight edge. Next, clamp the wheels up in the vice, using a metal distance piece between them and bolt right home. The float of a big end is not of great importance provided that there is at least 0·005 in. clearance.

The fly-wheel assembly may now be revolved between centres, and the trueing up process commenced with the aid of a scribing block. Before going further it is as well to add that the possession or access to the above-mentioned articles is absolutely essential, otherwise the job must not be attempted. It is best to concentrate on the mainshaft as near the wheels as possible, and, if the work has been carried out successfully so far, the shafts should be dead true. A heavy lead hammer will be required to shift the wheels when the high spots come opposite to one another. It should not be necessary to remind the reader that the fly-wheels should on no account be struck while in the centres. Mark the high spot with chalk, remove wheels from centres, place them on the bench and, while striking them, tilt over slightly with one hand. A wheel may only be struck at a point about 90 per cent round the rim from the crankpin. If high spots come in the same position on both shafts, the wheels should be pinched in the vice over that position. When doing this job a great deal of patience is required, but the reader will find that dead accuracy at this point will be more than repaid. It should not be found necessary to loosen the crankpin nuts each time. The author would like to point out that if the reader has no means of grinding the big end bush internally at hand the best plan is to return the connecting rod to the works.

After the fly-wheels have been successfully trued up and while they are still in the centres, the bearings may be fitted to the engine shafts. The bearings should be rather a tight sliding fit. If they are too tight, the shafts may be eased down with emery cloth, at the same time revolving the wheels. If the bearings are fitted too tight (especially in the case of the ball bearings), it will be impossible to locate end play in the shafts when the crankcase is bolted up. We next come to the fitting of the bearings in the crankcase. The old bearings may be removed by first warming the case and then dropping it down on a flat wood surface, causing

THE ENGINE

the bearing to jar from its position. Make sure there are no pieces of metal lying about to damage the face of the case, and it should not be found necessary to heat the latter beyond the boiling point of water. The new bearings should just slide in with the case fairly warm. If they are definitely too tight, the bearing housing can be carefully scraped until the desired fit is obtained. Should the bearings be driven in with great force, it will be found extremely difficult to remove them, and, more important still, the bearing ring may be caused to contract to such an extent as to cause an overload on the balls or rollers, and lead to premature failing of the bearing. On the other hand, the bearing may be too loose in the housing and in this event there are two methods of fitting available. Firstly, the edge of the crankcase housing can be caulked with a flat punch, the section of which may be $\frac{3}{4}$ in. × $\frac{1}{2}$ in., with the bottom filed to the contour of the housing. This must be done with the bearing in place, and every care should be taken to see that the operation is not carried to the extent of causing distortion in the bearing. The second and probably the most satisfactory method is to tin the outside of the bearing. While the soldering iron is heating, hold the bearing near the flame. This is most easily accomplished with the assistance of a piece of wood pushed into the centre. The bearing is ready to take the solder when the flux is just on the point of sizzling. Utmost care must be taken over the preliminary, and during, soldering to see that the bearing does not overheat and discolour. In this event it is best to "scrap" it and buy another one. The latter is a fairly expensive procedure, so it therefore behoves one to watch points. Touch the solder with the iron and make this sufficient to go right round the bearing. Watch the colour intently and keep the iron on the move all the time. Any irregularities in the tinning must be removed. Although much has been said on fitting bearings to the crankcase, it will be found that these extreme measures are rarely necessary owing to the care which is bestowed by the manufacturers on the fitting and machining of the crankcase when turned out originally. The next procedure is to ascertain the end play in the mainshafts. Assemble the flywheels in the case and bolt up.

A true judgment of end play can only be made if all the bolts are in. Give each end of the mainshaft a smart tap with the copper hammer to settle things down. Grasping the case in one arm, lightly tighten one end of the mainshaft between the vice clamps. By alternately pulling and pushing the amount of end movement will be apparent. The end play can be between 0·004 in. and 0·01 in., according to the use to which the engine will be put. The smaller figure, 0·004 in., is sufficient for a side valve touring engine, while 0·01 in. is about right for a Model 90 or an engine required to "rev." Should the end play require adjustment, shim washers must be used, and these are supplied by the makers in varying thicknesses. If the shafts are of the riveted-in type, the washers may be put in the shafts before the bearing. The other pattern, in which the shafts are of the tapered fit type, there will be a radius at the base of the shaft. In this case the washers must be put between the double bearing on the driving side. When all the above operations have been completed it is only necessary to

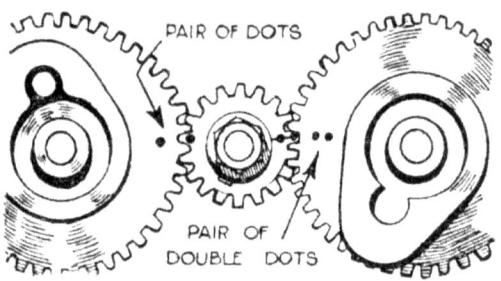

FIG. 25. THE MARKING OF THE TIMING PINIONS
The inlet cam wheel is on the left and the exhaust cam wheel on the right
(*From "The Motor-Cycle"*)

carefully clean both faces of the crankcase, smear with a jointing compound or gold size, and finally bolt the two halves together.

With regard to the fitting of new bushes for the rocker-levers and timing cams respectively in the crankcase and the timing cover, it is advisable to have this done at the works, as a large variety of reamers and special spot cutters are necessary if this work is to be carried out with any degree of success. The same also applies in the case of fitting new engine shafts to the flywheels, as almost invariably it will be found that a special shaft has to be fitted, and this can only be done successfully at the works.

If the foregoing instructions are properly carried out and assuming the reader to be a competent mechanic (if not, the work should on no account be attempted), a first-class job is assured.

Valve Gear. The timing gear on the Sunbeam is very straightforward and is illustrated in Figs. 25 and 26. The inlet and exhaust valves are each operated by a separate cam wheel, and these, together with the cam levers, work in phosphor-bronze bushes situated in the crankcase and timing cover. These bushes, provided they are well lubricated, will last indefinitely. The cam levers interpose between the cam and the tappet in the side valve.

while in the case of the overhead valve models, the ends are hollowed out to take the push-rods, the tappet adjustment being

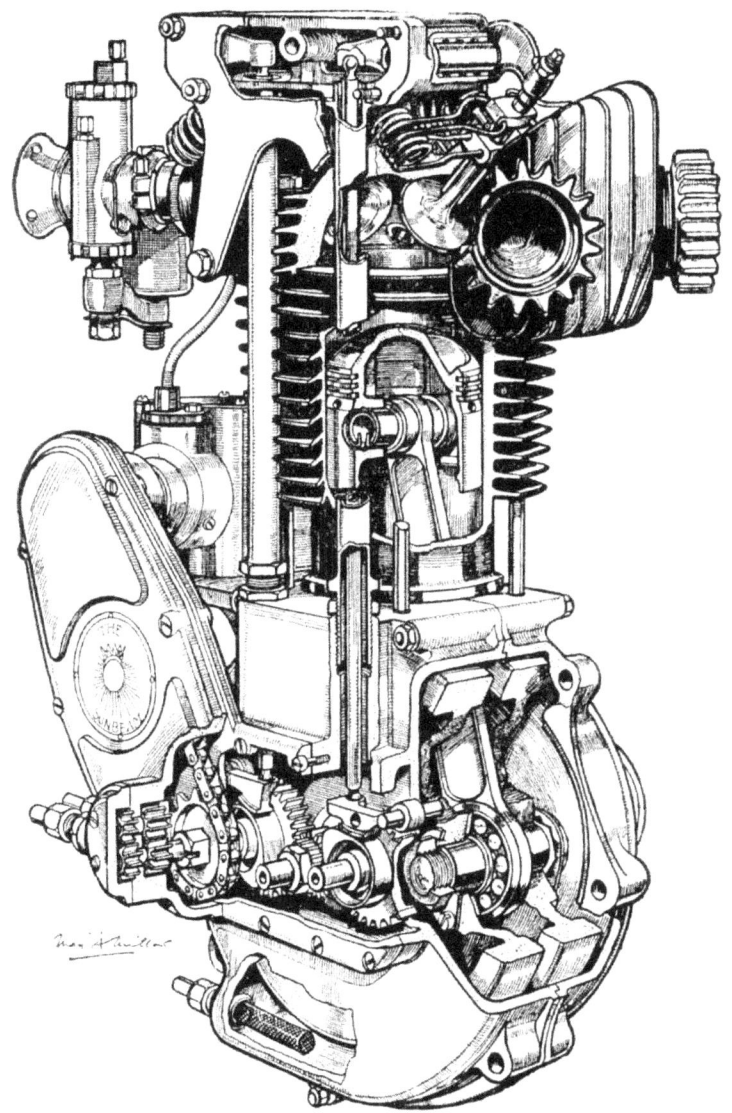

Fig. 26. A Partly Sectioned View of 1930 Sunbeam Engine
(*From "The Motor-Cycle"*)

effected direct to the valve stem. As the timing gear is being constantly fed with oil, a considerable period will elapse before any replacements become due, but should the rockers and cam faces show signs of wear or grooving to any extent they should be renewed. If the wear is not excessive, the faces may be "skimmed up."

If for any reason the timing gear is dismantled, the retiming of the valves is a comparatively simple matter. The small central pinion is keyed to the engine shaft and therefore cannot alter. One of its teeth has a single punch mark, and another tooth has either two punch marks or a line. The inlet cam has a gap between two teeth marked with a single punch mark, and the exhaust cam has a gap marked with either two punch marks or a line. Replace the inlet cam so that the tooth with one mark enters the gap with one mark, and, without disturbing the central pinion, similarly replace the exhaust cam so that the tooth with two marks or line enters the gap with two marks or line.

The makers do not recommend any deviation from the above straightforward valve timing, as this has been adopted after much careful experiment, and there is, consequently, no advantage in replacing otherwise than as marked.

Magneto Timing. It is a popular fallacy amongst the less experienced motor-cyclist that advancing the ignition timing will increase the speed. This is not so and a too early magneto timing is definitely harmful to the engine. The makers have determined by careful experiment the most suitable magneto timing for each individual engine and these are given herewith—Model 10, $\frac{5}{16}$ in. or 30°; Lion Models, $\frac{7}{16}$ in. or 35°; Model 9, $\frac{9}{16}$ in. or 43°; Model 90, $\frac{5}{8}$ in. or 50°. The magneto should be timed when the platinum points are about to separate with the magneto control at *full advance*. The above figures refer to the distance at which the piston should be before top dead centre, the last one in each case being in degrees for the benefit of those who prefer the dial marking method. The Model 90, being a special racing machine, may be given more latitude with regard to magneto advance and, if used for racing, the distance may be increased to $\frac{3}{4}$ in., but the latter necessitates a fuel mixture of 60 per cent benzole and 40 per cent petrol. If used for track work with a special high compression piston and using special alcohol fuels such as P.M.S.2 or R.D.1., the engine will stand a magneto advance of up to 1 in. To alter the timing, remove the aluminium cover in the chain case by sliding the spring to one side. This gives access to the magneto-driving pinion. Remove the sleeve-nut and in place of it screw the special extractor tool provided by the makers. If this is screwed right home and a sharp blow given on the end, the driving pinion will free itself. Make sure that the piston is at the top of the compression and not the exhaust stroke when timing. This may be verified by noting that both valves are fully closed with the normal clearances at the tappets or rockers, according to the type employed.

The platinum points should be kept adjusted, so that when separated by the cam to their fullest extent, the gauge on the magneto spanner (equal to approximately 0·012 in.) will just slip between them.

CHAPTER IV
GEAR-BOX AND CLUTCH

WHEN carrying out the following instructions with regard to adjusting and overhauling the gear-box, the author would like to point out that they apply to three entirely different types. The standard three-speed sliding pinion gear-box has been practically unaltered since its inception, and the instructions given herewith are applicable to all models from 1921 to 1933, except of course the $4\frac{1}{4}$ h.p. Model 7. The instructions given for the cam-operated gear-box apply to the $4\frac{1}{4}$ h.p. up to 1930 and in their main essentials to the 1933 type four-speed gear-box.

The main differences between the two are that on the three-speed gear-box the gears are changed by means of a sliding pinion moving on the mainshaft, while in the case of the four-speed the various gears are engaged by means of a camshaft which moves dog clutches through the agency of swivel plates.

GEAR-BOX (SLIDING PINION TYPE)

Adjustment of Control. To check the adjustment, put gear lever into neutral notch, turn back wheel, and bring lever slowly from neutral towards low gear position. Note exact point at which gears are first heard to touch. Then repeat the operation, moving lever towards middle gear and again note point at which gears first touch. Finally, note the point which is exactly equidistant from the other two. If this central point does not coincide exactly with the neutral notch, detach the upper yoke on the operating rod from the change speed lever, loosen the lock-nut and turn the yoke as necessary. If the central point is on the *low* gear side of neutral, screw yoke farther *down* the rod. If the central point is on middle gear side, screw the yoke farther *up*. Finish by tightening lock-nut on yoke.

To Remove Gear-box. Detach both chain cases and chains. Unscrew nuts on studs supporting clutch bridge and slide bridge off the studs, taking care not to lose any of the nine balls from the inner end of the ratchet lever. These balls must be packed into the lever with a little grease when re-assembling. Detach yoke at lower end of gear control rod from gear operating lever. Detach union at gear-box end of oil pipe. The gear-box is then free from all attachments and will drop out of its lug on removal of the two large nuts on the ends of the attaching studs.

GEAR-BOX AND CLUTCH

When replacing, make sure of chain tension, gear control adjustment, and clutch control adjustment.

To Dismantle Gear-box. If dismantling the gear-box is necessary, first detach gear-box sprocket. The nut is held by a locking plate and screw. Then remove cover. The high gear pinion will come away with the latter. Unscrew small set-screw in striking fork and unscrew gland-nut on side of gear-box. The shaft (and the operating lever attached to it) will then pull out sideways. The gland nut can be used for forcing the shaft out of the striking fork, by holding a flat spanner between nut and lever while unscrewing the nut. But first remove set-screw. Lift out striking fork and sliding pinion. Lift out layshaft. To withdraw the mainshaft it is necessary to remove the clutch and then knock out the two long keys on outer end of shaft. To detach the high gear pinion from the cover, it is necessary first to drive out the two keys. The ball bearing will remain in the cover.

To re-assemble, first replace mainshaft with keys. Insert layshaft with bigger end downwards. Replace striking fork and sliding pinion together, the sliding pinion with smaller end downwards and fork with set-screw upwards. Insert shaft for fork so that the recess for set-screw comes exactly opposite the screw and screw up the latter. Also screw up gland-nut outside the casing. Replace the high gear pinion in cover and insert keys. Before replacing the cover, make sure that both faces are absolutely clean, and smear the surfaces with gold size or seccotine. Then put on cover, tighten up all cover nuts, replace sprocket, tighten nut, fix locking plate, and insert screw for latter.

GEAR-BOX (CAM-OPERATED TYPE)

Adjustment of Control. A mark is cut in the sliding rack which operates the gears. This mark must be visible outside the gear-box when the change-speed lever is in neutral (free engine position). There are two nuts on the operating rod, one each side of the eye-piece on the rack. By setting these nuts higher or lower on the rod, the rack can be drawn into correct position. Leave these nuts quite tight after adjusting. Always check this setting any time that the gear-box has been moved.

To Remove Gear-box. Detach both chain cases and chains. Unscrew nuts on studs supporting clutch bridge and slide the bridge off the studs. Next, take off the nut on the control rod from *below* the eye-piece on the rack and slip the rod out of the eye-piece. Detach union at gear-box end of oil pipe. The gear-box is then free from all attachments and will drop out of its lug on removal of the two large nuts on the ends of the attaching studs.

When replacing make sure of chain tension, gear control adjustment, and clutch control adjustment.

To Dismantle Gear-box. Unless the reader is a fairly skilful mechanic he would be well-advised to leave the gear-box, with the exception of the periodical greasing, well alone, particularly as trouble in the box invariably gives ample warning of its approach by a distinct " groaning " or " whining " noise. For those, however, competent enough, the following instructions will be of assistance. Some of the earlier machines were fitted with a three-speed cam-operated gear-box, and the instructions apply to these as well as the old type four-speed and, in the main, to the present type four-speed.

From clutch end of mainshaft remove kick-starter centre piece and knock out the two long keys. Detach gear-box sprocket from cover. Its nut is held by a locking plate and screw; all right-hand threads. A $\frac{5}{16}$ in. box spanner should be used on the recessed nut of the cover. The high gear pinion comes away with the latter, but can be removed from it if its two keys are first knocked out. The ball bearing is a press-in fit and must not be disturbed.

Remove the various pinions from the shell in the following order. First pull out the spindle which holds the two striking forks in position and with it push the lower fork out of its groove in the camshaft on the side farthest away from the layshaft. Work upper fork out of its grooves and lift it out. With an indelible pencil or piece of chalk mark it as the upper fork and also mark which side was uppermost as it was assembled. Next, lift the double dog clutch off mainshaft. Take the small inspection lid off the side of the box and, with finger inserted through opening, lift lower (double) dog clutch into engagement with middle gear pinion. Turn the pinion until the dogs will engage. If the mainshaft and pinions are slightly raised, the layshaft, together with the lower fork, can be extracted.

Mark this as the lower fork and also mark which side was uppermost as assembled. All forks are interchangeable but after use they will naturally go together again most easily in the way in which they have been run in.

The mainshaft can now be carefully knocked out from the clutch side of the gear-box, together with the rest of the pinions. For purposes of re-assembling, note the difference between the two dog clutches and the middle and low gear pinions. The low gear is the smaller. The tubular piece with splines is the low gear sleeve. The large disk is the oil retaining washer.

There is seldom any need to remove the camshaft from the box, but when this is necessary, first slip off small pinion (which fits

GEAR-BOX AND CLUTCH

over a key). Then rack and shaft can be withdrawn. Do not disturb any of the bearings or bushes.

To Re-assemble Gear-box. Replace camshaft with keyed end uppermost. Slide in the rack with teeth towards camshaft. The gap between the third and fourth teeth is marked with a punch mark. Fit the small pinion on camshaft with projecting boss downwards. The third tooth clockwise from the key-way is marked with a punch mark. Turn camshaft so that small pinion will fit on to the key with the marked gap. Now push rack into gear-box to the extent of four teeth and keep it in this position during the whole process of re-assembling the remaining parts.

Next, hold mainshaft upright, screwed end uppermost, and slide on the middle gear pinion, dogs uppermost. Push on low gear sleeve with smooth end uppermost and push it right home on the mainshaft, firmly down on to the pinion. Put on the double dog clutches and turn middle gear pinion till the dogs intermesh. (Find the position in which the dog clutch is an easy sliding fit on the splines of the sleeves.) Next, put on low gear pinion, dogs downwards. This leaves a very small projecting edge of the sleeve, on which put the oil retaining washer.

Now replace mainshaft with all the above pieces into the gear-box. Take great care that the oil-retaining washer remains on the end of the sleeve and not merely lies loose on the shaft. The best way is to fix the mainshaft in a vice and fit the gear-box down on to it till the shaft is right home. Then the washer is bound to be in its correct place.

Now turn the gear-box the other way up and support it in this position, so as to leave both hands free. Then replace parts in the following order. First fit lower fork into groove of double dog clutch, and next proceed to fit third gear pinion, dogs downwards, on the mainshaft, second gear pinion dogs upward, sleeve smooth end uppermost, double dog clutch, low gear pinion dogs downwards and then the oil-retaining washer. Fit rack and cam in gear-box and then replace mainshaft and parts, noting the warning about the position of the oil-retaining washer. Now fit lower fork with projection upwards, layshaft (this entails slightly lifting the mainshaft and parts, with probable displacement of the oil-retaining washer, *in which case it must be worked back into its proper place*), double dog clutch, and upper fork, with projection downwards, and finally the fork spindle, pushing the latter right home.

Replace high gear pinion in cover and fit its keys. Before fitting the cover and inspection lid, clean all faces and smear the surfaces with gold size or seccotine. Also put half a teacupful of engine oil into the gear-box, poured well all over the various parts. Then put on cover and lid, tighten up all nuts and screws, replace gear-box sprocket, tighten nut, fit locking plate, and insert screw.

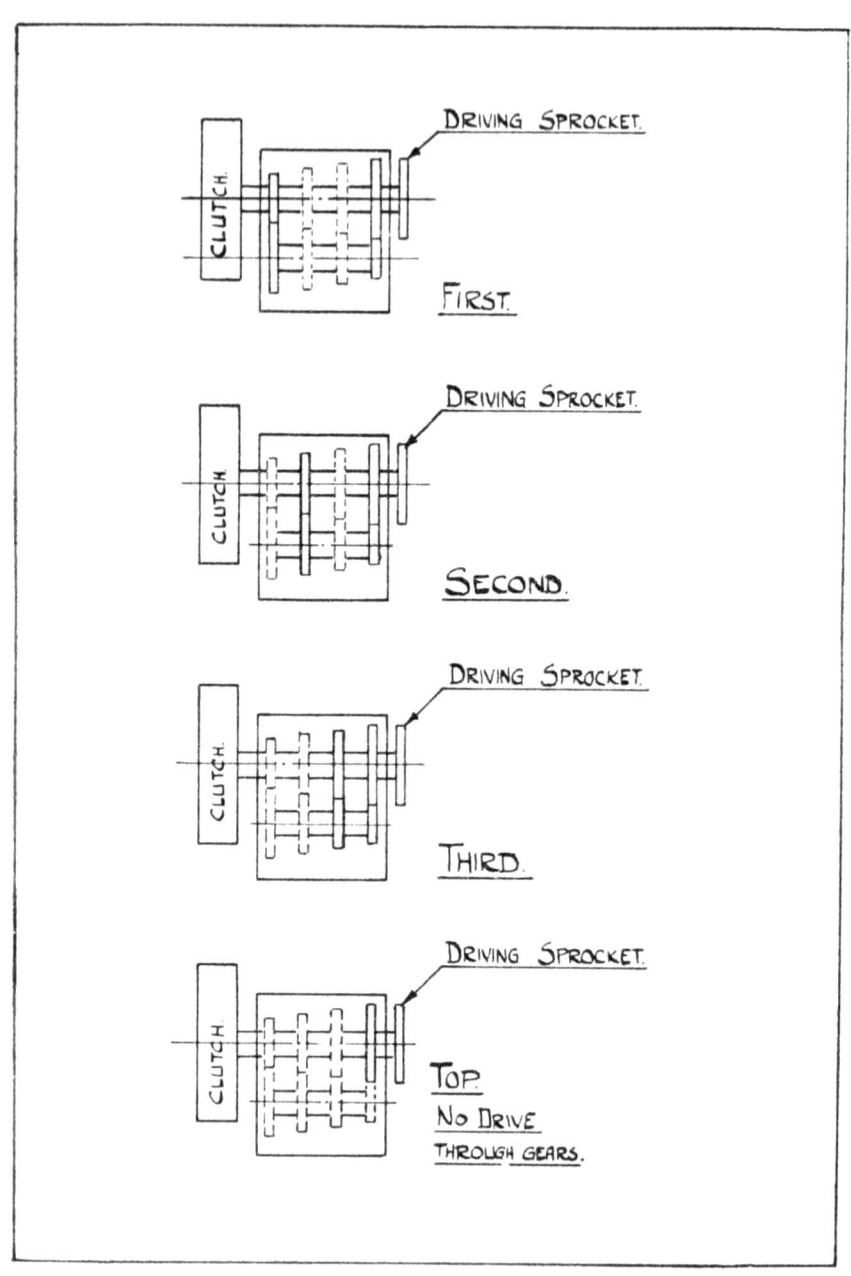

Fig. 27A. Showing how the Various Gears are Meshed

These final operations are not easy at the first attempt; they are simply a matter of exactitude. *On no account use any force whatever.* Once the correct position is found, the spindle will push right home without fuss. Finally fit long keys to clutch end of mainshaft and put on kick-starter centre piece, which completes the re-assembling process.

The following instructions will assist especially the owners of the 1932 Model Lion 9 and 90, which employ four-speed gear-boxes. A diagram showing how the various gears are meshed is given in Fig. 27A.

The last part to be fitted in the box before fitting the cover is the toothed quadrant which operates the revolving cam. The cam pinion has one of the teeth marked with a dot. A similar dot is placed opposite one of the tooth spaces of the quadrant. When fitting the quadrant in place, these two dots must come together, otherwise the various gears will not engage properly. When the cover is fitted and the box is in position on the machine, fit the lever loosely on the serrated end of the quadrant spindle. Revolve the gears slowly by hand and turn the quadrant in a clockwise direction, as far as it will go. This will engage the low gear dogs in the box. A small movement of the quadrant in the opposite direction, i.e. anti-clockwise will put the gears into neutral position. The spring plunger in the bottom of gear-box will give the exact location. Without removing the quadrant, now remove the operating lever. Then set the gear lever on the tank in the neutral notch of gate plate, i.e. first notch from top end. Then fit the operating lever to quadrant spindle in such a position that gear rod will connect up at each end, without moving either the quadrant or the gear lever on tank. If the exact position cannot be obtained, the gear rod will have to be readjusted for length. This is done by slacking off the lock-nut under the joint piece at top end of rod and turning the joint piece either up or down as necessary, afterwards tightening up the lock-nut.

THE FOUR-SPEED BURMAN

A partly sectional view of the Burman constant-mesh four-speed gear-box is shown in Fig. 27B. The functioning of the box may be easily understood by reference to the illustration and to the various letters given in the text. The box is used up to 1939.

Gear-box Operation. The *modus operandi* of the gear-box may be followed by reference to Fig. 27B.

(1) *First Gear.* The gear is disengaged from pinions B and D and the sliding clutch W moves to the right and engages with pinion G. The drive is taken through the clutch A to the mainshaft T, to sliding gear C, to pinion G, to clutch W, to V, to

pinion E, to main gear B, to chain sprocket J, and via the rear driving chain to the rear wheel.

(2) *Second Gear.* In the case of the second gear, the sliding clutch W moves to the left and engages with pinion F. The drive is taken through the clutch A to mainshaft T, to the larger gear

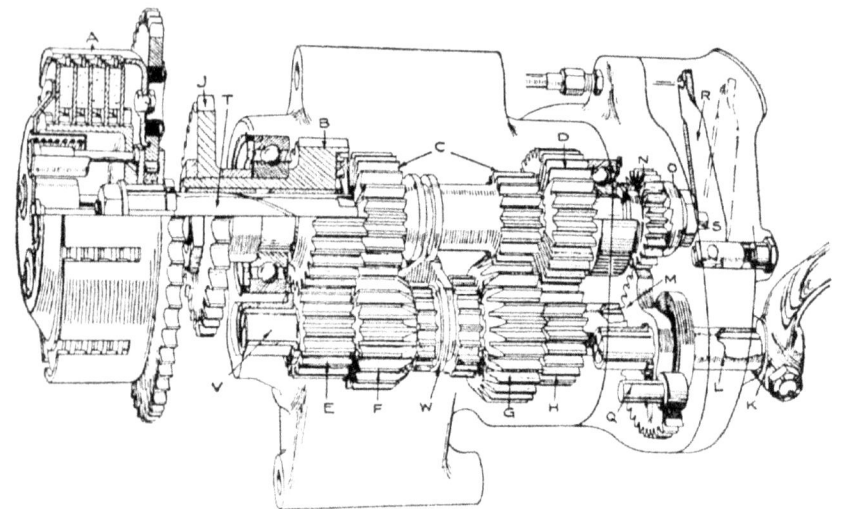

FIG. 27B. BURMAN FOUR-SPEED GEAR-BOX AND CLUTCH

A.	Clutch assembly.	L.	Kick-starter axle.
B.	Main gear wheel.	M.	Kick-starter quadrant.
C.	Mainshaft sliding gear which has a pinion at each end.	N.	Kick-starter ratchet pinion.
		O.	Kick-starter ratchet drive.
D.	Mainshaft third gear.	P.	Kick-starter return spring
E.	Layshaft small pinion.	Q.	Kick-starter stop.
F.	Layshaft second gear.	R.	Clutch-operating lever.
G.	Layshaft first gear.	S.	Clutch thrust-rod.
H.	Layshaft third gear.	T.	Gear-box mainshaft.
J.	Final-drive sprocket.	V.	Layshaft.
K.	Kick-starter crank.	W.	Layshaft sliding clutch.

on sliding gear C, to pinion F, to clutch W, to layshaft V, to pinion E, to main gear B, to chain sprocket J, and thence to the rear wheel.

(3) *Third Gear.* When third gear is in use, the sliding clutch on the layshaft remains disengaged from pinions F and G and the sliding gear on the mainshaft moves to the right and engages with pinion D. The drive is taken via the clutch A to mainshaft T to sliding gear C, to pinion D, to pinion H, to layshaft V, to pinion E, to maingear B, to chain sprocket J, from which the power is transmitted to the rear wheel by the driving chain.

(4) *Fourth Gear.* When top gear is in action the sliding clutch on the layshaft remains in the position shown (Fig. 27B), i.e. disengaged from pinions F and G. The sliding gear on the mainshaft

moves to the left and engages with main gear *B*. The drive is taken through the clutch *A* to mainshaft *T*, to sliding gear *C*, to main gear *B*, to chain sprocket *J*, and lastly by the final drive to the rear wheel.

Camshaft and Selectors. *B* in the selector forks *C* and *D* (Fig. 28) engage in the profiled grooves cut in the shaft *A*. The forks *C* and *D* engage in the sliding gear, individually, on the mainshaft

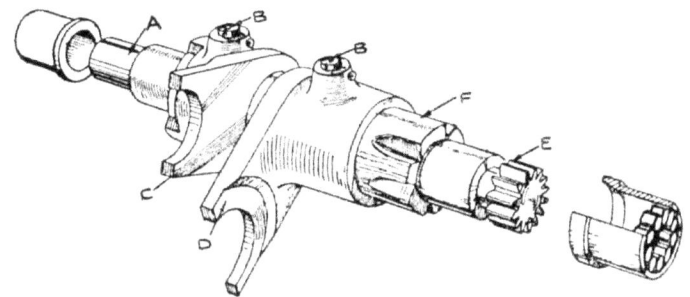

Fig. 28. Burman Camshaft and Striking Forks

and the sliding clutch on the layshaft. Thus the forks are permitted to slide sideways, which movement is controlled by the profiled cam grooves cut in the shaft. Partial rotation of the shaft will set up the endways sliding movement. Integral with the shaft is the small pinion *E*, which meshes with the toothed sector on the foot gear-control mechanism. Cut in the shaft are the notches *F*, which are employed to accommodate a spring-loaded pawl which positively locks the gear in any of the desired gear positions.

Gear Jumping Out. If after extensive use there is a tendency for the gear to jump out, it may be due to any of the following causes—

(*a*) Weakening of the spring operating the pawl in the gear-box shell.

(*b*) Wear on the ratchet in the foot-change mechanism.

(*c*) Excessive wear on the two bushes in the main gear pinion.

Kick-starter Ineffective. Possible causes of a defective kick-starter are—

(1) *Jamming*. Should the kick-starter jam, this is probably due to wear on either or both of the quadrant teeth and the ratchet pinion. A temporary repair may be effected by filing the

teeth. If the first tooth of the quadrant is damaged, this may be filed in order to give a lead.

(2) *Slipping.* This is caused by a stripped quadrant or worn ratchet teeth.

(3) *Crank not Returning.* Should this trouble occur, renewal of the return spring invariably effects a remedy.

Gear-change Lever. Should the foot gear-change pedal not

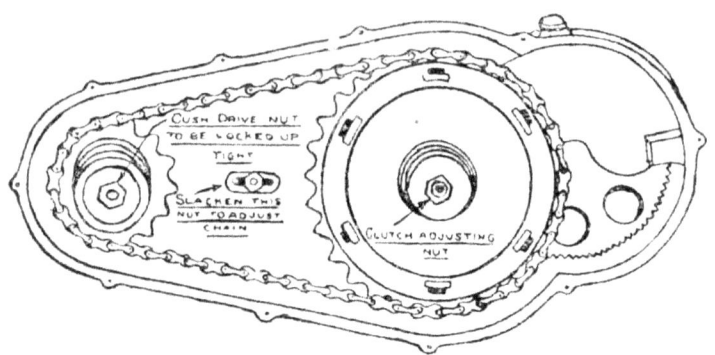

Fig. 29. The Front Chain Case (1928)

return to position, the centralizing spring will most likely be at fault.

CLUTCH ADJUSTMENT

The various forms of clutch adjustment are detailed below. The later machines have only two adjustments, those given in *b* and *c*, while the machines up to 1928 have only one central spring to create pressure, and this is adjusted by means of the large nut in front of the spring as shown in Fig. 29.

(*a*) Keep the screw in the centre of the gear-box bridge, Fig. 30, adjusted to the point that there is just an appreciable slack in the operating lever which hangs down below the bridge. To ascertain if there is any slack at this point, it is advisable to detach the shackle by which the clutch cable is attached to this lever. It is only necessary to undo one screw. The adjustment is effected by loosening the large lock-nut on the clutch bridge and the screw in the centre is screwed in or out as required. See Figs. 30 and 31. The adjustment is correct when the lever has just a little play (about $\frac{1}{8}$ in.) when the cable is detached. When the adjustment is correct, be sure to tighten the lock-nut. On the Model 90, a knurled knob supplants the above and the adjustment can be made by the fingers only.

(*b*) When (*a*) is correct, excessive slack in the operating cable can be taken up on the small adjuster screwed into the front of the gear-box bridge. Set this so that a small amount of movement can be felt at the operating lever on the handlebars when the clutch is engaged. On machines fitted with adjustable clutch

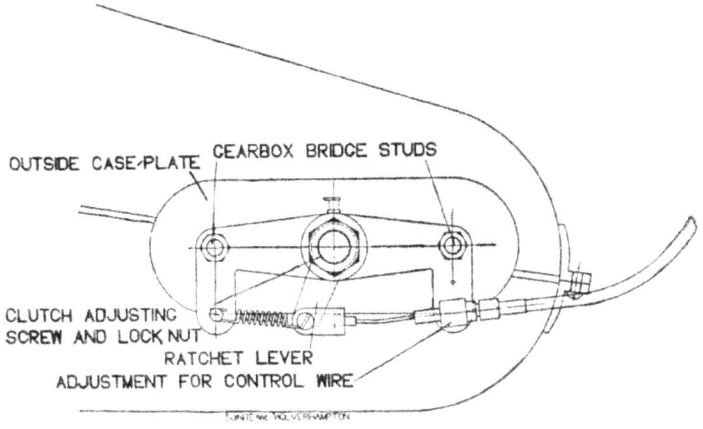

Fig. 30. Clutch Bridge

stops in the front chaincase, care must be taken not to adjust the cable too tightly, otherwise the clutch would come home against the stops before the clutch plates had separated enough to allow of changing gear, and thus cause damage to the gear pinions.

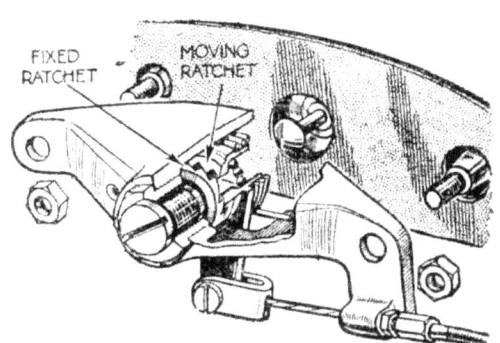

Fig. 31. Clutch Adjustment
(*From "The Motor-Cycle"*)

(*c*) Provided that (*a*) and (*b*) are correct, there should be no likelihood of further adjustment, but if there is insufficient tension on the plates it will be necessary to increase the spring pressure. The aluminium clutch dome, which is attached by four screws to the front chain case, should be removed to give access to the spring adjustment. First slacken each of the six lock-nuts, then screw down each of the adjusting nuts, making sure that each one receives an equal number of turns, and finally tighten up the lock-nuts when the adjustment is effected. *Do not* have this adjustment tighter than is necessary, as this will cause the clutch to be very stiff to operate. If at any time clutch slip should set in, always see that (*a*) and (*b*) are both correct before attempting to increase (*c*).

Removing Chain Case. To remove the front chain case, unscrew the sixteen small screws round the outer edge, when the outer half of the case will come away. In the event of it being necessary to remove the back half, dismantle the clutch as explained elsewhere. Remove outer nut, washer and spring of cush drive. The cush drive, chain and clutch sprocket will then come away together. Remove kick-starter segment and shaft. Next proceed to remove the cush drive centre piece by screwing in the special extractor provided by the makers. When the extractor is screwed right home, it should be given a smart blow, when the centre piece will free itself. Detach the three small screws with spring washers which attach the case to the gear-box shell. If the nut on the central stud is removed, the chain case will come away.

It should be noted that only machines later than 1922 have the detachable centre piece. On any machines previous to that date a sprocket drawer must be used. In case a sprocket drawer is not handy, a couple of wedges (a pair of long tyre levers answer the purpose) can be inserted between the crankcase and the centre piece. A good sharp blow on the end of the mainshaft will then loosen the centre piece. Be careful to use no more force than is necessary and do not damage the thread on the end of the shaft.

Reassemble in reverse order. The three small screws with spring washers must be made dead tight. Give the screwdriver a final turn with a spanner. The nut on the central stud must also be really tight. Make sure that the cush drive and clutch are both right home or the chain will be out of line. Before screwing on the outer half of the chain case, carefully clean the lips and smear them with gold size or seccotine so as to make an oil-tight joint.

Removal of Back Chain Case. Disconnect and remove the accumulator and oil tank from models so fitted. Remove the right-hand exhaust pipe and silencer on Model 9, together with the kick-starter crank, dust plates, and change speed rod.

Unscrew union nut which attaches small oil pipe to the release valve in the crankcase and pull the pipe out of the chain case. Slacken the nuts on the two studs supporting the clutch bridge. (The present machines are not fitted with this bridge.) Remove the two small screws in the angle lugs at each end of chain case;

GEAR-BOX AND CLUTCH 63

also the two bolts attaching lower half of chain case to the frame. Lower half will now drop away. Arrange the spring link of the driving chain so that when the case is removed the chain will sag on to the stay.

If it is desired to remove the top half also, take out the two bolts attaching case to frame. The top half will now pull out forwards and upwards. Removal of either bottom or top half is rendered easier if the detachable rear wheel is first removed.

When replacing, make sure that both case plates (at gear-box end) are *outside* and that all lips are correctly entered. The easiest way is first to replace the top half; then attach bottom half to top at *rear* end and see that the lips are correct. The fingers can then be slid along the joint whilst the front of the case is being lifted. The two halves of the case will then come together easily. Last of all tighten the nuts on the studs supporting the clutch bridge and replace small oil pipe.

Dismantling Clutch (Types up to 1928). There are two types of Sunbeam clutch, one with metal plates and one with cork insets. A certain amount of oil in either is no disadvantage—it keeps the metal plates "sweet" and prevents the corks from wearing. If, however, excessive oil gets into the clutch (i.e. too much is allowed to collect in the front chain case or so much is put into the gear-box that it flows out through the mainshaft bearing), the clutch should be washed out with paraffin, to accomplish which, proceed as follows.

Drain out surplus oil through drain plug. Replace plug and pour in half a pint of paraffin through inspection cap and replace plug. Put machine on back stand and start engine. Put top gear into engagement, keep engine running slowly and keep lifting and releasing clutch lever so as to separate the clutch plates. Then carefully drain out the paraffin and lubricate the chain with a little engine oil.

To dismantle the cork clutch, remove outer half of chain case and chain, take off outer nut, washer and spring of clutch, remove lock-nut on mainshaft and the fixing nut behind it, slide off outer plate and slip operating key out of its key-way. The rest of the clutch will then slide off the shaft and can be taken apart and cleaned. The metal plate clutch is dismantled in a similar manner, but slip off the outer plate before removing the fixing nut and lock-nut.

After cleaning, re-assemble the cork clutch in the following order.

First fit body (back plate) with boss downwards, then sprocket with slotted flange outwards, sleeve (central piece with splines) so that its key-way coincides with the key-way in the shaft, then fixing nut and lock-nut. Next replace plain (middle) plate with raised boss outwards and cork plate with raised side outwards. Certain cork clutches have two corked and two plain plates. These are put on alternately, starting with a plain plate next to the sprocket. Now engage low gear and turn wheel till key-way in mainshaft is parallel with the ground. Then insert operating key exactly centrally in the key-way and slide on outer plate so that the key enters the key-ways cut half way through the plates.

Finally, put on main clutch spring, washer and outer nut, and adjust spring pressure.

In the case of the metal plate clutch, first lay the back plate on a table with its projections upwards. Then place the plates on it, steel and bronze alternately, starting and ending with steel. The bronze plates have places cut in them to engage with the projections on the back plate. The steel plates have projections to engage with slots cut in the flange of the sprocket. Bring these projections into line and then put on the sprocket over them, flange downwards, so that the projections engage in the slots. This encloses all the plates between the back plate and the sprocket. The complete assembly is then pushed on to the mainshaft sprocket outwards. (The ratchet piece of the kick-starter, if it has been taken off the mainshaft, must first be replaced, ratchet teeth outwards, so as to engage with the ratchet ring on the back plate.) Now push the sleeve on to the shaft. The keys on the sleeve have been ground off at one end; put this end on first, i.e. next to the sprocket. Then put on fixing nut, lock-nut, key (as described for cork clutch), outer plate, spring, washer and nut, and finally adjust spring pressure.

To Dismantle Clutch (1928 and Later Types). Remove outer half of front chain case. Take out the six split pins and undo the lock-nuts and adjusting nuts in the clutch centre piece. The springs can then be taken off and the outer plate with thimbles will come away (Fig. 32). A large lock-nut holds the clutch centre piece on, and before this can be removed the thin locking washer must be flattened out. Should this washer be damaged, obtain a new one, as it is essential that the lock-nut should be prevented from turning. The best way to undo the lock-nut is to put the machine in gear and hold the footbrake on, when the nut may be removed with the aid of the box spanner provided by the makers. The centre piece can then be drawn off together with the clutch sprocket. When reassembling it should be borne in mind that the lips on the steel plates should face outwards. The 1928 and early 1929 machines were fitted with $\frac{1}{4}$ in. studs in the clutch centre piece, and if the transmission is subjected to severe shocks these may be found to break.

To overcome this difficulty, the author would suggest fitting a set of the later pattern heavy $\frac{5}{16}$ in. studs, as these will stand practically any strain. To fit these, drill out the centre piece

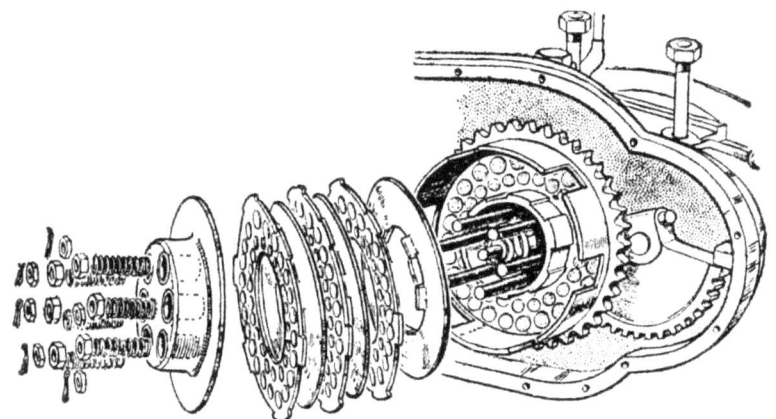

Fig. 32. 1928 Sunbeam Clutch Dismantled
(*From "The Motor-Cycle"*)

to take the new size stud. Place a piece of hollow tubing over the stud to bear on the shoulder and rivet-snap or punch over the end of the studs. When the larger studs are fitted it will be realized

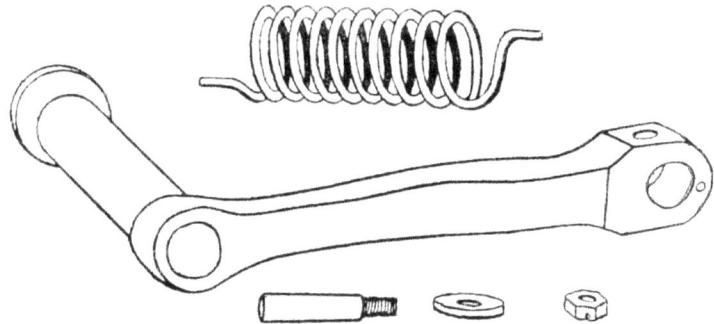

Fig. 33. Kick-starter Dismantled (Early Type)

that a set of new adjusting nuts together with lock-nuts will be necessary.

Kick-starter Mechanism. Should the kick-starter mechanism be maltreated, i.e. jumping on the crank, forcing it when not properly in mesh or starting with the ignition too far advanced causing a backfire, it may be found necessary to dismantle it.

To Remove Crank. Take the nut and washer off the cotter-pin (Fig. 33), and knock the latter out, taking care not to damage the thread. The crank and return spring are then free and can be slid off. If stiff, withdraw by winding in a clockwise direction.

To Replace Crank. Slide on the return spring and fit one end into a hole drilled in the bottom of annular recess round the shaft bearing. Slide on crank in such a position that the other end of the spring can be fitted into the hole drilled in the back of the crank. Wind the crank in an anti-clockwise direction until it is vertical and replace the cotter-pin and nut. The end of the shaft should come level with the face of the crank. Should the shaft be found to move when pushing on the crank, tap lightly on the face of the latter. This will enable the shaft to be drawn into position.

To gain access to the kick-starter ratchet pinion, the clutch must be dismantled, as described elsewhere.

Should either the loose ratchet or the one on the back plate show any signs of being badly chipped, it is advisable to replace them both. The fixed ratchet is screwed on the back plate and then held in position with two pegs. The 1930/1 machines have a loose ratchet piece which slides on the mainshaft instead of the fixed one on the back plate. If, on examination, the first one or two teeth on the kick-start segment are damaged, it is permissible to grind them off and thus enable the segment to give further service. It will be realized that this grinding off process shortens the travel of the kick-starter and, therefore, if many of the teeth are damaged a new segment will be required.

CHAPTER V

COMPONENTS

THE cycle parts, by which is meant, the forks, hubs, brakes, etc., require adjustment and replacement from time to time, and these will be dealt with in the following order.

Forks. Although quite a number of different type forks have been employed by the makers, the adjustments necessary apply to practically all models. The main point to bear in mind is that wear in the fork spindles is almost entirely due to lack of lubrication. Therefore *grease well and often*.

To take up wear on the top rear bearing pin, slacken nuts on both ends of the pin and screw it *clockwise*, farther into the right link by means of the thin hexagon inside the left-hand link. Screw right up and then slacken back fully one half-turn and tighten the nuts again at both ends of the pin. The top front pin carries the multi-plate shock absorber shown in Fig. 34, and this requires no adjustment. This pin is prevented from turning by the nut outside the left link which must be kept tight. To take up the play in the bottom bearing pins, slacken the nut on the left end of the pin and turn the hexagon at the right end in a clockwise direction. Screw up sufficient to take up the slackness and then lock by tightening nut on end. It is essential that the fork adjustments be kept in perfect order, otherwise the steering will be seriously affected.

Shock Absorber. A hand-adjusted shock absorber, Fig. 34, is incorporated in the front forks and should be adjusted in the following manner. For normal riding it can be run either loose or slightly tightened. For fast work over really bad roads, it should be adjusted considerably tighter. If it is necessary to dismantle the shock absorber, first take off the small nut and washer outside the knob. The knob can then be unscrewed. (Some models have a sleeve nut which passes through the centre of the knob and to prevent any possibility of the aluminium thread stripping, screw the absorber knob up tight). The plates and friction disks will then be free to slide off. To reassemble, first put on a friction disk, then a plate which anchors on the stud in the fork girder, next a friction disk, then a plate anchoring in the absorber itself, and so on alternately. Make sure that the two square studs are screwed up true to the square holes in the plates.

Otherwise the latter will bend and not move when the knob is tightened or loosened. Do not disturb these studs unnecessarily.

Two other patterns of shock absorber are in use, firstly, the type which has large friction disks between the shackle plates, and, secondly, the B. & D. Stabilizers. These should be adjusted so that the fork springs can just comfortably return to their normal

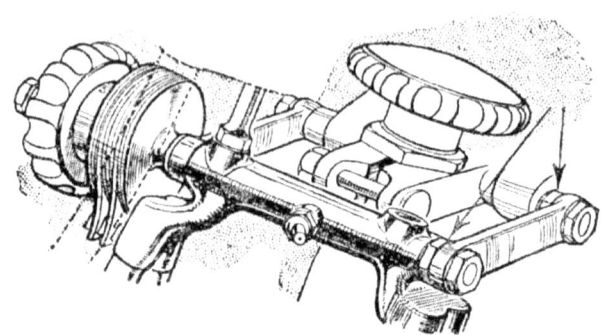

FIG. 34. THE FRONT FORK LINKS
(*From "The Motor-Cycle"*)

position after being compressed. The B. & D. have large wing-nuts to facilitate adjustment.

Steering Head. The two ball bearings in the head are packed with grease when assembled and should stay in adjustment for a considerable time. Should any looseness develop, however, slacken the nut on the cross bolt in the clip. Unscrew the steering damper knob and rod and tighten the large head nut in a clockwise direction with the special spanner provided. *Tighten the nut in the clip bolt* after the adjustment is complete or the handlebar will be loose. Do not adjust the head too tight or the steering will be affected.

Steering Damper. Owing to the exceptional steering on a Sunbeam, the steering damper need only be used on a sidecar outfit and for really high speed solo work. It is adjusted by turning the large black knob at the top of the steering head in a clockwise direction to tighten. When used with a sidecar, the damper should be screwed down fairly tight and this will prevent any tendency for the handlebars to swing from side to side. For solo work, tighten the damper when going fast over bumpy roads and then not beyond the point at which the machine corners naturally, and without conscious effort in turning the handlebars. When slowing down after a high speed "blind," remember to loosen the damper, otherwise the machine will become difficult to handle.

If the damper needs to be dismantled at any time for the renewal of the friction disks, bear in mind that the bottom back fork bearing pin must be removed, as this passes through the steering damper body.

Wheels. All the larger, that is all except M. 10 1932 machines, are fitted with detachable and interchangeable wheels, and con-

Fig. 35. The Quickly Detachable and Interchangeable Rear Wheel

sequently the adjustment of the hub bearing is identical. The various other types of hub bearing will be dealt with later.

To Remove Front Wheel (1932). Put the machine on both stands (Fig. 35), take the nut and washer off the knock-out spindle when the latter may be withdrawn. A large knurled knob is provided to assist this operation. The distance piece and washer between the hub and fork should drop out. Remove the three square-headed pins which lock the hub to the drum. A special tube spanner, shown in Fig. 36, is provided by the makers to fit these pins. The wheel should then be pulled towards the left-hand side, enabling it to slide off the splines and be removed. This method of removal also applies to the rear wheel and to the rear wheels only of all machines from 1928 onwards, when the drop-out rear wheel was first instituted.

TO ADJUST FRONT AND REAR HUBS

Interchangeable Wheels. A pair of special spanners with oblong holes are provided in the tool kit for adjusting the hub bearings. The larger one fits the cones on the rear wheel sleeve and the smaller one fits the lock-nut for the adjusting cone. Hold the

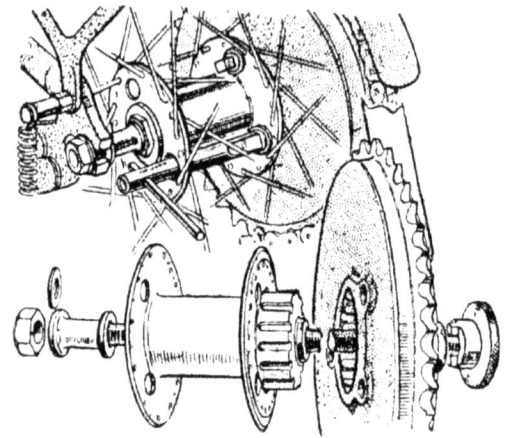

FIG. 36. DETAILS OF THE ASSEMBLY OF THE QUICKLY DETACHABLE REAR WHEEL
(*From "The Motor-Cycle"*)

adjusting cone with the large spanner and loosen the lock-nut in an anti-clockwise direction with the small spanner. Next, with the large spanner, hold the fixed cone at the other end of the sleeve and adjust the moving cone by screwing in an anti-clockwise direction. After the bearing has been adjusted, hold the moving cone with the large spanner and tighten the lock-nut in a clockwise direction. (It should be noted that the lock-nut has a right-hand thread and the adjusting cone a left-hand.) Take care not to adjust the bearing too tightly. Screw up till all looseness is just lost and then slacken back a quarter of a turn. Check the adjustment after the wheel has been replaced in the machine and the nut of the knock-out spindle has been tightened home, as this will tend to further tighten the wheel bearing. When all the nuts are tight the wheel should spin freely without any appreciable slack.

To Remove Front Wheel (1926-31). Detach the brake rod from the operating lever by unscrewing the yoke pin and nut. Remove the pin anchoring the brake plate to the right-hand fork side, and slacken the two nuts at the ends of the front wheel spindle. By prising out the two inner washers from their recesses, the front wheel will be allowed to drop out.

To Adjust Front Hub. Loosen nut on left-hand end of spindle and turn cone as necessary by means of the double-ended spanner. Screw clockwise to tighten. *It is essential that the hub bearings are not over-tightened* as this causes rapid "pitting" of the cones. The

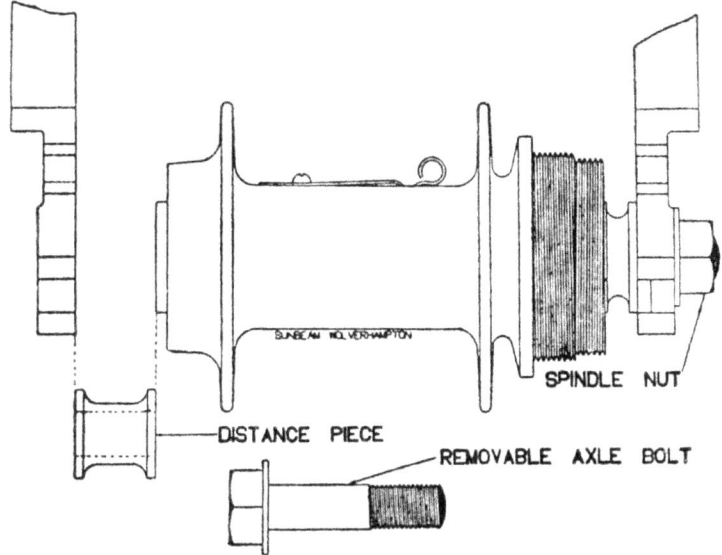

Fig. 37. The Divided Rear Axle

action of tightening the nuts on the ends of the spindles naturally presses the cones together by the amount of play in the threads. Therefore, only just take out excessive play when adjusting and make sure that the wheel spins perfectly freely after all the nuts have been finally tightened.

Removal of Divided Rear Axle Wheel. Many Sunbeams up to 1927 are fitted with the Sunbeam patent divided axle shown in Fig. 37. The object of this is to enable the inner tube to be removed if a puncture is experienced without the need for the removal of the wheel. If the detachable axle bolt at the left-hand end of the wheel spindle is removed together with the distance piece, it is a comparatively simple matter to remove the tube and, if need be, the cover, and thus effect any tyre repairs with the wheel *in situ*. Should it, however, be necessary to remove the whole wheel, proceed as follows.

Remove chain, which of course necessitates the removal of the rear chain case on models so fitted; then slacken nut on right-hand end of wheel spindle, when the wheel will slide out of the slotted fork ends. On the machines with internal expanding brakes, the rod or cable must be detached from the operating lever on the brake cam. To adjust the wheel bearing, slacken the axle bolt on the left-hand side of the machine and also the spindle nut on the right-hand side. The cone on the right-hand end is pegged to

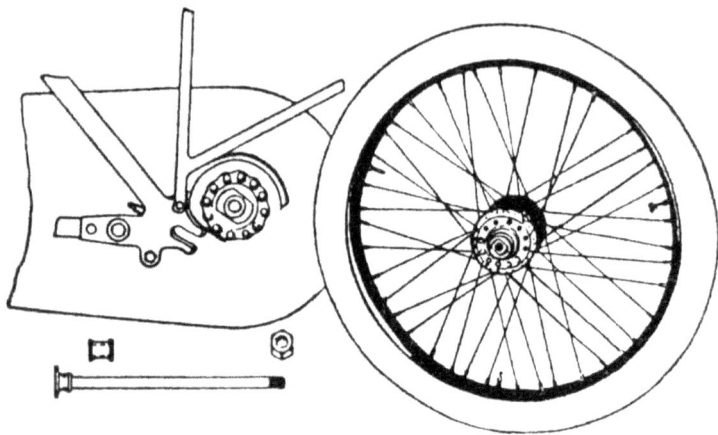

FIG. 38. THE DETACHABLE WHEEL

the fork end and the bearing is adjusted by turning the rest of the wheel spindle. Two flats are provided on the spindle which should be turned in a clockwise direction to tighten.

Earlier Interchangeable Wheels. Fig. 38 shows the principle of the earlier type interchangeable wheels which is very similar to the present-day pattern, with the exception that the three hub pins and splines replace the pegs and holes previously used. The method of hub bearing adjustment is precisely the same as that described for the later models.

Brakes. Both brakes on the 1932 machines are of the internal expanding type—7 in. in diameter—and each of these remains in position when the wheel is removed. The adjustment necessary to keep the brakes in perfect working order is dealt with elsewhere, but should it be necessary to remove the brake for any reason, proceed as follows—

As the method is very similar for both brakes the rear only will be dealt with. First remove the rear wheel and rear chain case (if fitted). The rear end of the cable is attached by a yoke and screw to the brake operating lever. To remove the latter, undo the nut about three threads and give the end of the spindle a tap. This will enable the operating lever to be taken off the serrations in the cam spindle. Take care not to damage the thread on the cam. Now unscrew the two large ¾ in. plated nuts; one on the bush in which the lever works and the other on the sleeve through which the removable wheel spindle passes. As both of these nuts are rather inaccessible with an ordinary spanner, a special spanner is supplied by the makers. The complete brake and sprocket can now be withdrawn. To remove the shoes, put the operating

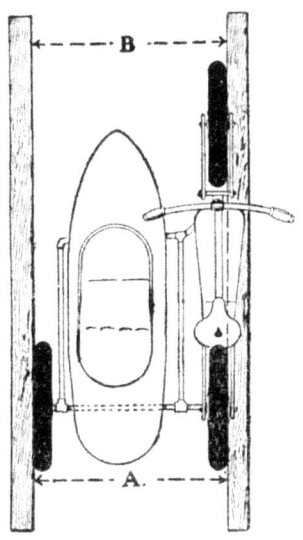

Fig. 39. Checking Wheel and Sidecar Alignment by Means of Boards placed along the Edges of the Tyres

lever back so that the cam may open the shoes to their fullest extent and insert a screwdriver between the brake plate and the shoe. Ease the latter away from the plate until the spring tension is lost, when the shoes and springs can be detached. Should the linings appear to be glazed or in a greasy, oily condition, they should be roughened with an old hacksaw in the first case and soaked with petrol in the second. If the linings are thoroughly greasy, it may be necessary to scrub them thoroughly with the above mentioned petrol and a good stiff brush, but do not attempt to burn the oil off by setting the linings alight. After the machine has covered a considerable mileage, the brake linings will need to be renewed. This is a straightforward job, hardly requiring description here, but the following will be of assistance.

Make sure that the copper rivets are countersunk well below the surface of the linings. A good tip which enables this to be done with less risk of weakening the fabric is to countersink slightly the holes in the shoe itself, as well as the lining material, so that the linings are well down on the shoes, and it is often wise to level off the fabric. Sometimes it is necessary to "bed" the liners down by running the machine on the stand in bottom gear and applying the brake fairly hard. When re-assembling, make sure that the cam spindle is quite free and that the passage from the grease nipple is not blocked up. Apply a smear of grease to the spindle, to the cam itself and also the fulcrum. Bear in mind that one's life may depend upon the brakes, and it is therefore of the utmost importance that these components should be kept at maximum efficiency.

Sidecar. All the Sunbeam models with the exception of the Model 10 are quite essentially capable of taking a sidecar, and when sent out of the factory these are carefully aligned to the motor-cycle. Special connections which fit into lugs on the frame enable the sidecar to be detached without disturbing the alignment. If, however, by accident or otherwise, the connections become altered, the sidecar must be very carefully re-aligned, otherwise severe and totally unnecessary stress will be imposed on the machine.

The method of lining up a sidecar is shown in Fig. 39. Two straight edges are required, one touching the sides of the tyres on the machine and the other touching the edge of the sidecar tyre. The distance between the straight edges A and B should then be measured, and the measurements at B should be arranged to be $\frac{3}{4}$ in. less than that at A, as it is found in practice that a combination steers much better if the sidecar wheel is allowed to run in a little, and also prevents any tendency for the machine to pull to the left.

It is sometimes found that while the sidecar is tracked up correctly a certain amount of drag is still discernible, and this is almost invariably due to the fact that the machine is not absolutely vertical.

To check this, place the outfit on level ground and take measurements from the front forks as indicated in Fig. 40. A straight piece of wood should be rested against a given point on the forks and the distance between its lower extremity and the centre of the front tyre should be measured. This distance is represented by C in Fig. 40. A similar operation should then be carried out on the other side of the machine when the two distances should be found to coincide. In the event of either of the measurements varying, the sidecar chassis should be adjusted in order to bring the machine in a dead vertical position. As the majority of one's driving is done on the left camber of the road, it will be found advantageous if the outfit as a whole is allowed to have a tendency to run to the right rather than to the left.

COMPONENTS

The makers fit and recommend a flexible ball joint to the rear connections and this should be kept adjusted to the point where there is *absolutely no play*, but not tight enough to prevent the ball from moving. If there is a considerable amount of play, the ball will hammer away both the socket and castellated ring. If too rigid, additional stress is placed on the rear fork end of the chain stay, which in time may cause the latter to fracture. Special spanners are provided to fit the ball joint, castellated socket, and also the lock-nut. In some cases, where the sidecar is used for extra heavy duty an additional connection, generally known as a "fourth point," will be an advantage, and this is generally fixed to the front down tube.

When the correct alignment for the sidecar has been obtained, it is most important to see that all the nuts are dead tight.

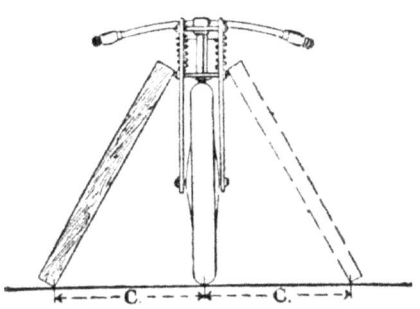

Fig. 40. If a Sidecar Machine is Vertical the Distances "C," Shown Above, should be Equal

Tyres. Continual tyre trouble will mar the enjoyment derived from the best of machines, so that attention to them will be well repaid. It is of primary importance that the tyres should be kept inflated to the right pressures, and these are given below.

Tyre Pressures

Model 10, 25 in. × 3·00 in.: front, 17 lb.; rear, 23 lb.
Models 9, 90, and Lion, 26 in. × 3·25 in.; front 16 lb.; rear, 19 lb.
Models Lion and 9 (600 c.c.), 26 in. × 3·50 in.: front, 16 lb.; rear, 16 lb.
Model 90, 27 in. × 2·75 in.: front, 23 lb.

Check the pressures up about once a fortnight by means of the gauge supplied by the makers of the valve—Messrs. A. Schrader & Sons. Avoid under-inflation like the plague. Running the tyres at too low a pressure causes a tremendous strain on the tyre walls and results in the casing eventually cracking, thus making the tyre useless, although the tread is still fit for further service. If habitual pillion work is indulged in, run with the rear tyre at a slightly higher pressure to compensate for the additional weight. Forestall trouble in respect of punctures by regularly examining the tyres and removing any sharp flints, pieces of steel or glass which inevitably find their way into the covers. Should a cut extend right through the tyre fabric, it should be vulcanized or filled with tyre stopping, otherwise, wet will find its way in and rot the fabric. When the machine is to be left standing for a long period, i.e. if the tax is not taken out for the last quarter of the year, both the wheels should be clear of the ground in order to prevent the weight of the machine being placed on one point of the tyres. Do not let the tyres stand in a pool of oil or paraffin as this will cause the rubber to soften and rapidly ruin them. Never forget to carry an efficient repair outfit, because a puncture mended any-old-how with a carelessly stuck-on patch is almost sure to give trouble at some later date.

When a wired-on cover has been removed in order to effect repairs, it is of extreme importance to make sure when replacing it that the whole cover runs truly. If this precaution is neglected, the steering will be affected. Take special care not to strain the wires by using large car type tyre levers when removing and replacing the cover. If the following points are borne in mind no difficulty should be experienced. To take cover off, completely deflate inner tube and pinch edge of cover right down into the base of the rim exactly opposite the valve. The cover should then be able to be removed at the valve without using any force. When replacing, very slightly inflate tube and put cover on first opposite the valve. If the edge is kept well down in the rim all the way round, the cover will slip on at the valve without force. Then half inflate and make sure that the edges go into their proper place all the way round on both sides of the rim. Spin the wheel and test for true running of the cover before and after fully inflating. Any inaccuracies can generally be rectified by striking the cover a judicious blow with the closed fist.

If the above points are borne in mind and unnecessary strain, such as rapid braking and fierce acceleration, are avoided, the tyres should last for a very big mileage.

Sparking Plug. It is not generally appreciated what an important part is played by the sparking plug, and too often the policy of using an unsuitable type or a worn plug, is adopted. It is best to fit only the types recommended. The specified types (see also page 103) for the different models are—

	LODGE
M. 10	H. 1.
"Lion"	H. 1.
M. 9	H. 1.
Ninety	H.L.S.
1937 S.V. Models	H. 1.
1937 O.H.V. Models	H. 14.
1939 Models B29, B30	C. 14.
All other 1939 models	H.L.N.

COMPONENTS

A special racing plug is fitted to the Model 90 and, as this will oil up very easily unless the throttle is kept open fairly wide, it is advisable to replace it with a standard plug. As the special racing plugs are considerably more expensive than the standard type, it is best to only use them for actual racing or high speed touring.

It has been found practically impossible to produce a plug which combines the two virtues of withstanding extreme heat and, secondly, refusing to oil up. That is the reason why the manufacturers design a plug which will withstand the high temperature generated in an engine under racing conditions.

There are various ways in which trouble may develop in a sparking plug and these are enumerated below.

Oiling or Sooting Up. It may be found occasionally that oil is deposited on the plug and causes it to cease sparking. This is caused by the oil mist which is always present in an engine, particularly when cold, condensing on the plug and so short-circuiting the current. It is seldom of much use just wiping the oil off the points and it is usually better to dismantle the plug and give it a thorough clean as illustrated in Fig. 41. The above trouble is most likely to happen when the machine has been left standing for some considerable time, allowing the oil to accumulate in the sump, and it is therefore advisable to drain the sump in order to eliminate the possibility of this occurring. After a considerable time, carbon deposit forms on the plug points and the surrounding cavity in a similar way to that of the cylinder head, and although the plug will continue to fire, if the deposit becomes excessive, the high tension current will take the line of least resistance and travel through the deposit instead of jumping the gap at the plug points.

Faulty Insulation. The insulation of the plug, composed of either porcelain or mica may develop a crack or some other defect causing the current to be "shorted." This latter trouble is fortunately somewhat rare, but when it occurs the only thing to do is to throw the plug away unless it is of the detachable type, when a new centre portion may be obtained from the makers.

Plug Point Gap. After a plug has been in use for a lengthy period, the points may be found to be eaten away by the continual sparking which takes place. This causes them to be too far apart and too wide a gap causes starting to be very difficult. The correct gap between the points should be 0·018 in.–0·020 in., and a gauge for setting the points to this dimension can be obtained from Lodge Plugs, Ltd., Rugby, or firms selling motor-cycle accessories. If the points are too far apart the wide electrode only should be bent towards the central electrode. A convenient method of doing this is with a pair of thin-nosed pliers.

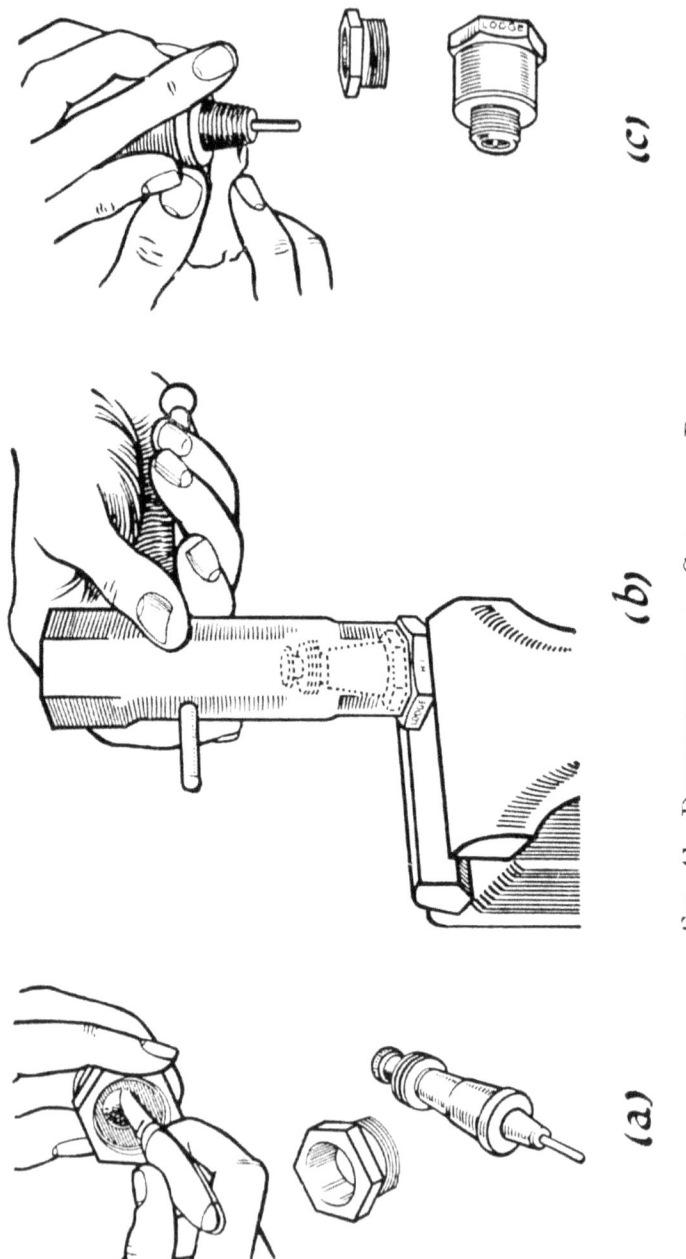

Fig. 41. Dismantling and Cleaning Plug

Plug Testing. The generally accepted method of testing the current at the plug is to place a wooden handled screwdriver across the terminal and lying close to the cylinder or any other metal parts. On rotating the engine a spark should be visible. The usual test for the plug itself is to lay it on the cylinder and note whether it sparks satisfactorily when the engine is turned over. A fairly good spark does not necessarily guarantee that the plug is O.K., as sometimes a plug will give off a fat spark under atmospheric pressure but fail to spark under the compression of the engine.

Cleaning the Plug. From time to time the plug should be removed and cleaned. The method of dismantling is shown in Fig. 41. If it is found in fairly good condition, it will be sufficient to wash the inside and outside with petrol. If, on the other hand, the points and the cavity surrounding them show evidence of much carbon deposit, it is advisable to clean the plug thoroughly. The centre portion bearing the main electrode may be detached by undoing the gland-nut. The carbon should be scraped from inside the body with the aid of a sharp penknife, and the main insulation should be lightly polished with a fine strip of emery, when the plug may be re-assembled. A non-detachable plug can only be cleaned by burning off the deposit as it is almost impossible to get a knife into the nooks and crannies. One method is to place the threaded part of the plug in the flame of a gas ring until it is dull red. Care must be taken not to get the plug too hot, otherwise the insulation may be irreparably damaged. The last tip need only be used for an expensive plug. The cheap non-detachable type should be thrown away.

THE CARBURETTOR

The various Amal carburettors fitted to the different Sunbeam models are each stamped with the initials indicating the type, e.g. the Model 90 carburettor is stamped M. 90 on the side of the body near the throttle stop. As, however, the principle upon which they work are identical, it will be sufficient to deal with one type. Fig. 42 gives a sectional view of the standard needle jet carburettor. A is the carburettor body or mixing chamber, B is the throttle valve to which is attached the tapered and adjustable needle C. The air valve D passes through the throttle valve and serves the purpose of obstructing the main air passage for starting and also the mixture regulator. Screwed to the mixing chamber by the union nut E is jet block F, between which a fibre washer is placed to prevent the possibility of petrol leaks. The specially designed adaptor body is situated on the upper part of the jet block and is designed to give a clear gas passage of high volumetric efficiency.

The pilot jet J is integral with the jet block and is supplied through the passage K. L is the adjustable pilot air inlet with its corresponding outlet passages, M and N. The needle jet O is screwed to the underside of the jet block and carries at its base the main jet P. Both the needle and the main jet may be removed when the jet plug Q is removed, as this bolts the mixing and float chamber together. The float chamber R, which receives the petrol supply at the bottom, is mounted on the platform S. The float T is contained in the chamber together with the needle valve U, attached to the float by means of the clip V. W is the float chamber top, which is screwed to the float chamber and prevented from loosening by the locking screw X. TS, which is shown in Fig. 42, is an adjustable throttle stop which enables the engine to continue ticking over with the throttle lever closed.

The sectional view of the adjustable pilot air screw is shown in the small, right-hand illustration, and will enable its method of adjustment to be fully understood.

THE AMAL NEEDLE JET CARBURETTOR

How it Works. The petrol tap having been turned on, petrol will flow past the needle valve U until the quantity of petrol in the chamber R is sufficient to raise the float T, when the needle valve U will prevent a further supply entering the float chamber.

The action of the float can readily be understood, for, as the quantity of fuel in the float chamber is used, the float T will drop, carrying with it the needle U, and admitting a further supply. Thus, automatically, the petrol level is kept constant. No alteration should be made to the standard petrol level.

The float chamber, having filled to its correct level, fuel passes along the passages, through the diagonal holes in jet plug Q, when it will be in communication with the main jet P and the pilot feed hole K; the level in these jets being, obviously, the same as that maintained in the float chamber.

Imagine the throttle valve B very slightly open. As the piston descends, a partial vacuum is created in the carburettor, causing a rush of air through the pilot air hole L, drawing fuel from the pilot jet J.

The mixture of air and fuel is admitted to the engine through the pilot outlet M.

The quantity of mixture capable of being passed by the pilot outlet M is insufficient to run the engine. The mixture also carries excess of fuel. Consequently, before a combustible mixture is admitted, throttle valve B must be slightly raised, admitting a further supply of air from the main air intake.

The further the throttle valve is opened, the less will be the depression on the outlet M, but, in turn, a higher depression will

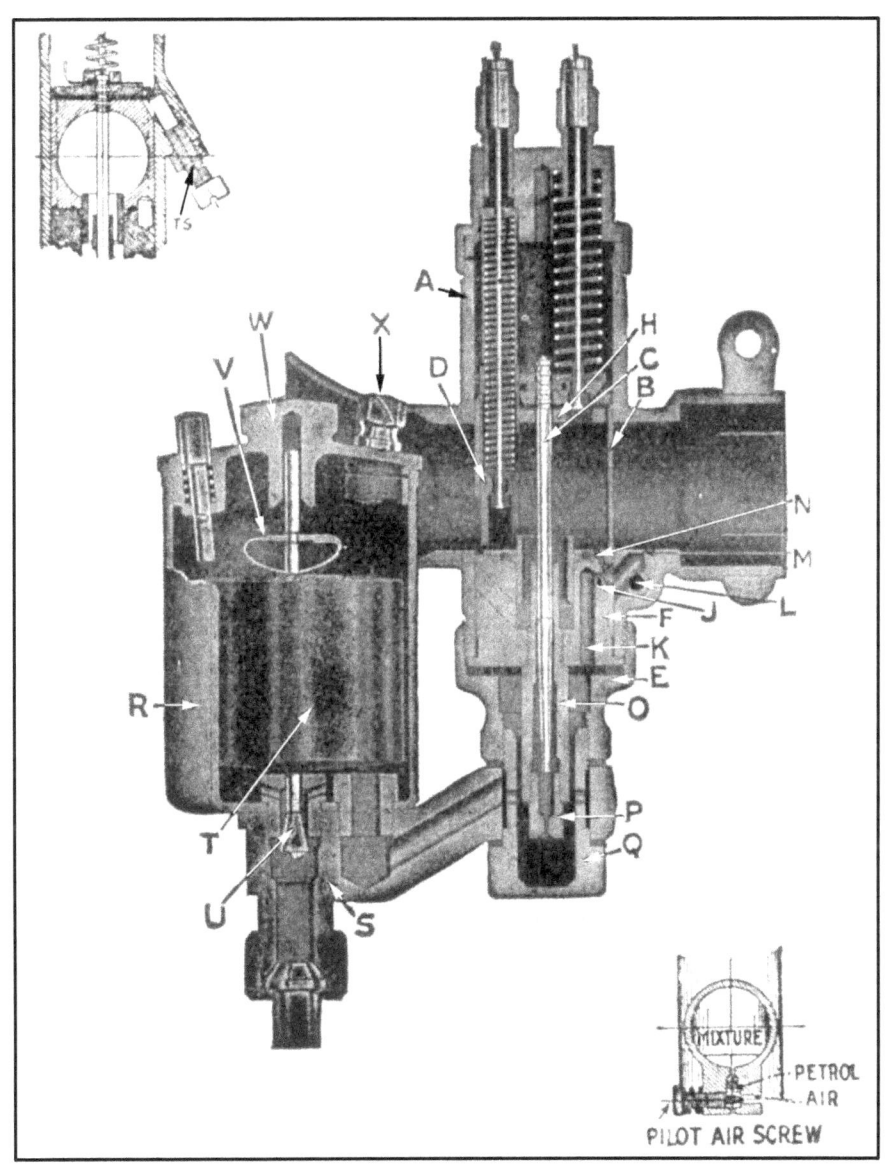

Fig. 42. The Amal Carburettor in Section

be created on the by-pass *N*, and the pilot mixture will flow from this passage as well as from the outlet *M*.

The mixture provided by the pilot and by-pass system is supplemented at approximately one-eighth throttle by fuel from the main jet system, the throttle valve cut-away governing the mixture strength from here to one-quarter throttle. Proceeding up the throttle range, mixture control by the position of the needle takes place from one-quarter to three-quarters throttle, and thereafter the main jet is the only regulation.

The air valve *D*, has the effect of obstructing the main through-way, and, in consequence, increasing the depression on the main jet, enriching the mixture.

Tuning the Needle Jet Carburettor. There are four ways in which the quality of the mixture supplied by the Amal carburettor can be varied, and these are given hereunder, in the order in which the adjustments should be made.

1. Main jet (three-quarters to full throttle).
2. Pilot air adjustment (closed one-eighth throttle).
3. Throttle valve cut-away on the air intake side (one-eighth to one-quarter throttle).
4. Needle position (one-quarter to three-quarters throttle).

The diagram, Fig. 43, clearly indicates the part of the throttle range over which each adjustment is effective. The carburettor having been carefully fitted, the general tuning can be carried out. The following sequence must be observed.

1. MAIN JET. *To obtain main jet size*, select the smallest size jet which gives the maximum speed. The air lever should be three-quarters open.

2. PILOT ADJUSTMENT. *To weaken slow running mixture*, screw pilot air adjuster outwards.

To enrich slow running mixture, screw pilot air adjuster inwards.

Screw pilot air adjuster home in a clockwise direction. Place gear lever in " neutral."

Commence by slightly flooding the float chamber by depressing the tickler until fuel can be observed overflowing from the mixing chamber. Set magneto at one-third advance with the throttle approximately one-eighth open, close air lever, start the engine and warm up.

After warming up, reduce the engine revolution by gently closing the throttle. The slow running mixture will prove too rich unless air leaks are present, so very gradually unscrew the pilot air adjuster.

The engine-speed will increase and must again be reduced by

gently closing the throttle until, by combination of throttle positions and air adjustment, the desired "idling" is secured. It is sometimes necessary to retard fully the magneto before good "idling" results, particularly when excessive valve overlap and very early ignition timing is employed.

Throttle Stop. If it is desired that the engine should continue "idling" with the throttle lever closed, the position of the throttle valve must be set by means of the throttle stop screw, the throttle

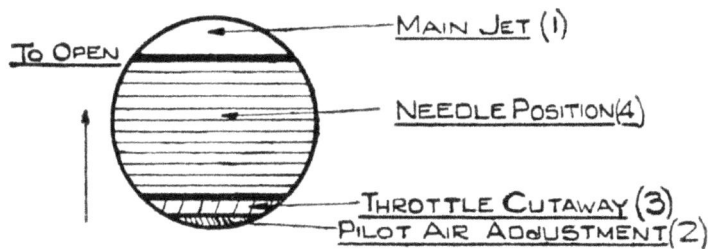

FIG. 43. RANGE AND SEQUENCE OF ADJUSTMENTS

lever being in the "closed position" during the adjustment. Alternatively, if the screw is adjusted clear of the throttle valve, the engine will shut off in the normal way by the control lever.

Do not take the throttle stop screw out completely.

Failure to secure good "idling" will probably be traced to one of the following causes.

Air leaks at the junction of the carburettor and engine, i.e. the carburettor being loose on the induction pipe or the induction pipe lock-nut not being tight enough. Excessive wear on the valve stems and guides or pitted valve seats, causing gas leaks. The sparking plug points may be oily or too close together. The remedy for this is explained elsewhere. Examine the contact breaker points and see that the gap is correct and the points clean. Remove the high tension lead and note that there are no signs of "shorting" and that the carbon brush is quite clean and free in its holder. If all the above are found to be perfectly satisfactory, then the trouble may lie in the magneto, in which case it should be returned to the makers or one of their service depots.

3. THROTTLE VALVE CUT-AWAY. Given satisfactory "idling," set the magneto control at half advance, air lever fully open. Very slowly open the throttle valve, when, if the engine responds regularly up to the one-quarter throttle, the valve cut-away is correct.

A weak mixture is indicated by spitting back through the air intake, with blue flames, hesitation in picking up which disappears when the air lever is closed down, and this can be remedied by fitting a throttle valve with less cut-away.

A rich mixture is shown by black smoke from the exhaust. Engine stops, or nearly stops, when the air valve is closed. The remedy for this is a throttle valve with more cut-away. Each Amal valve is stamped with two numbers, the first indicating the type number of the carburettor, and the second figure the amount of cut-away on the intake side of the valve in sixteenths of an inch.

Thus 6/4 is a Type 6 valve with $\frac{4}{16}$ in. or $\frac{1}{4}$ in. cut away.

The standard valve for single-cylinder engines is No. 5.

4. NEEDLE POSITION. Needle positions are counted from the top of the needle, and the groove nearest the needle top is No. 1. Open the air lever wide and the throttle approximately half way, and note if the exhaust note sounds healthy and the engine lively.

Close air valve slightly below throttle, exhaust note and engine speed should then remain practically unaltered. Should popping back and spitting, together with blue flames from the carburettor intake occur, then the mixture is too weak and should be made richer by raising the needle slightly.

Test by lowering air valve gently. Engine revolutions will rise when air valve is lowered slightly below the throttle valve.

If, on closing the air valve below the throttle valve, there is a tendency to misfire and eight-stroking, together with a smoky exhaust and heavy laboured running, the mixture is too rich and may be cured by slightly lowering the needle.

The normal needle setting is with the needle clip in No. 3 groove.

Having found the correct needle position, the carburettor setting is now complete, and it will be found that the driving is practically automatic once the engine is warmed up.

In order to obtain a semi-automatic setting, that is, when extreme economy is desired, lower the needle one groove farther after carrying out this range of tests, while for speed work, the main jet may be increased by 10 per cent when the air lever should be fully open when on full throttle. The following symptoms will act as a good guide in obtaining the correct carburettor setting.

Rich Mixture. General indications are: heavy thumpy running, emission of black smoke from the exhaust, the inside of the carburettor becomes blackened and, as the throttle is opened, heavy "blowback" of fuel is observed from the carburettor air intake.

Weak Mixture. Difficult starting, tendency for the engine to fire back through the carburettor, indicated by blue flames from the carburettor air intake. Carburettor becomes sensitive to the "drive" and constant use has to be made of the air lever, engine knocks readily and runs hot, with loss of power. The electrode of the sparking plugs shows indication of intense heat, and the mica insulation becomes white, polished exhaust pipes become rapidly blued.

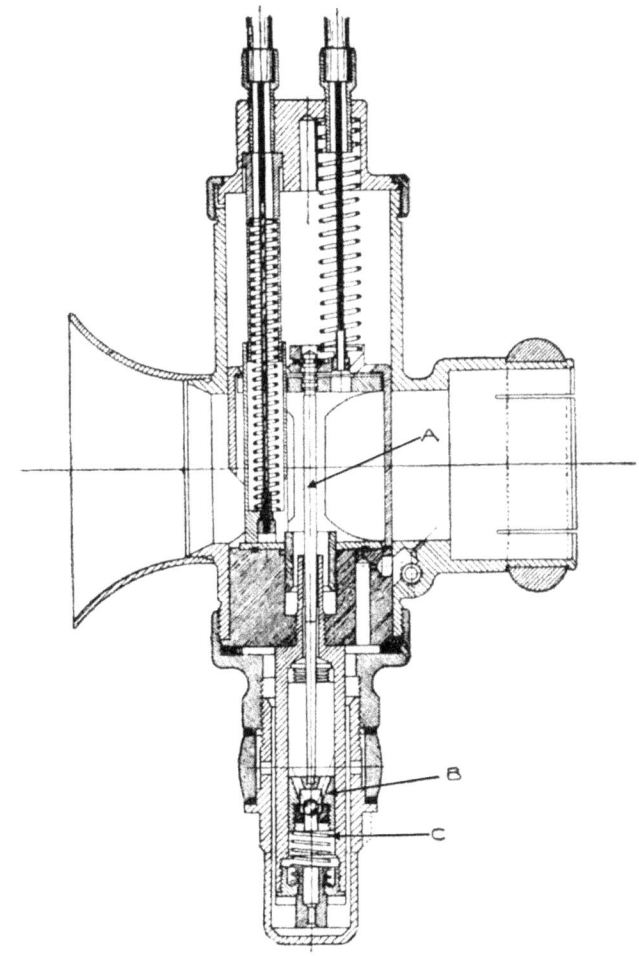

Fig. 44. Sectional Diagram of the Amal Carburettor with Pump Attachment Fitted

Tuning the Amal Acceleration Pump Carburettor. The Sunbeam is not fitted with the pump type carburettor (Fig. 44) as standard, but for the benefit of those owners who desire this very useful fitting, the following will be of assistance. With the pump in use, an additional tuning factor is introduced, namely, the stroke of the pump.

This is controlled by a distance collar which is situated at the top of the pump chamber.

The pump stroke which will give the best all-round results is that which is as small as possible but large enough to give the desired acceleration from slow speeds.

If, therefore, there is any suspicion of heavy laboured running when the throttle is rapidly opened, it is a sign that the pump stroke is too great and a thicker distance collar should be placed in the pump chamber.

In the event of spitting back taking place when the throttle is violently opened, this is a sign that the pump stroke is insufficient, and a thinner collar should be fitted in the pump chamber.

The existing collar is detached by means of an extractor tool which is screwed into the collar, thus enabling it to be pulled out, and the operation is reversed for the introduction of another collar.

It must be remembered that a controlling factor of pump stroke is needle position, and this must, of course, be determined in the normal way as explained previously.

All other means of tuning should be carried out on the pump type carburettor in exactly the same way as for the non-pump type.

Important Note. To start from cold, first open the throttle wide twice, then close to the best starting position. This primes the carburettor better than flooding. Do not open and shut the throttle unnecessarily when the machine is not running, otherwise you might overprime the carburettor. If you do overprime, open the throttle wide and give a couple of kicks; then close down again to the best starting position.

If you remove pump piston, see that you replace it the correct way up, that is, with the four holes at the top.

Tuning the Amal Track Racing Carburettor. The tuning to the track racing carburettor, which is included for the benefit of the racing enthusiast, is carried out in three stages, as follows—

1. The main jet (three-quarters to full throttle).
2. Pilot screw (closed to one-eighth throttle).
3. Throttle valve (one-eighth to three-quarters throttle).

The tuning should be carried out in the order mentioned, and is exactly the same as for the needle jet carburettor described earlier in this chapter, except, of course, paragraphs referring to the needle jet.

The condition of the sparking plug should be carefully observed each time a trial is made. A dry baked appearance is an indication of weak mixture, or alternatively, of an unsuitable grade of plug.

Fifty per cent increase in mixture strength is obtainable by means of the air control, thus—if intelligent use is made of this, there is no chance of "cooking" the engine due to weak mixture.

Idling and slow running are controlled by the adjustment of the pilot air screw which, for petrol fuel, should be unscrewed two and a half turns and for alcohol half a turn.

A No. 12 valve is the normal size for all types of carburettors, but due to variation in valve timing and engine design, this can sometimes be varied, giving improved acceleration.

It is unnecessary to alter the valve cut-away when changing from petrol to discol or any similar alcohol fuels. The makers recommend that twin-float chambers should be used with alcohol fuels on engines of 350 c.c. and upwards. Fuel pipes should not be less than $\frac{1}{4}$ in. in diameter.

Maintenance of the Amal Carburettor. To maintain the efficiency of the carburettor, you are strongly advised to periodically clean it. This is best done by entirely dismantling and washing each part in clean petrol, and in so doing the following points should be observed—

If the jet block is tight, it should be tapped out by means of a wooden stump in the mixing chamber. Renew any worn parts, as: needle valve, if the head has a distinct ridge at the point of seating; throttle valve, if excessive side play is present; mixing chamber union nut washer, if worn or damaged; taper needle and clip, if it is possible to rotate the needle freely in the clip.

Be sure that all pilot passages are clear; this is done best by inserting a fine bristle.

In re-assembling, no brute force is necessary. Make sure that the taper needle is re-fitted in correct groove, securely locked by its clip, and that it enters the hole in top of jet block. See that the needle valve enters the top of float chamber cover easily, and that mixing chamber is fitted vertically and pushed right home on engine stub. Ascertain that the needle valve clip V registers correctly in its grove. Probably it will be found necessary to re-set the pilot adjusting screw, and this should be carried out as previously mentioned.

CHAPTER VI
ELECTRICAL SYSTEMS

THE Lucas "Magdyno" which, as its name implies, consists of two units. The magneto which attends to the ignition and the dynamo which looks after the lighting is now almost universal. As shown in Fig. 45A, the dynamo portion of the unit is now detachable so that the "enthusiast" who wishes to enter his Sunbeam for racing or competition work can easily remove all the lighting equipment. A suitable fitment is supplied by the makers which protects the gears when it is desired to run the machine without the dynamo. The dynamo, as will be seen, is mounted above the magneto, and is driven by gears from the magneto spindle, the direction of rotation being anti-clockwise. The current output to the battery is regulated by two main brushes, the positive of which is insulated and the negative earthed. To these must be added a third brush which is provided on the underside of the commutator bracket which controls the output at high speeds, thus keeping it within safe limits.

Dynamo. If the dynamo cover has to be removed for any reason, *disconnect the positive lead of the battery* to avoid the danger of reversing the polarity of the dynamo or short circuiting the battery, either of which might cause serious damage. The lead from the positive battery terminal is connected to the lead from the switch by means of a brass connector. To disconnect, remove the rubber shield and unscrew the cable connector. Care must be taken that it does not touch any metal part of the frame as this will short circuit the battery. When connecting up again, do not forget to pull the rubber shield over the connector.

Brushes. If for some reason it is necessary to run the machine with the battery removed or disconnected, it is advisable to remove the brushes. This is easily accomplished by holding the spring lever aside. The spring lever is shown at P (Fig. 45A.) If the brushes are in good condition, they should slide quite freely in their holders and make good contact with the commutator. Should the brushes be found in a dirty or greasy condition, clean them with a cloth moistened with petrol. If after considerable service the brushes become so worn that they will not bear properly on the commutator, they should be replaced. It is advisable to fit only the brushes supplied by the makers as these

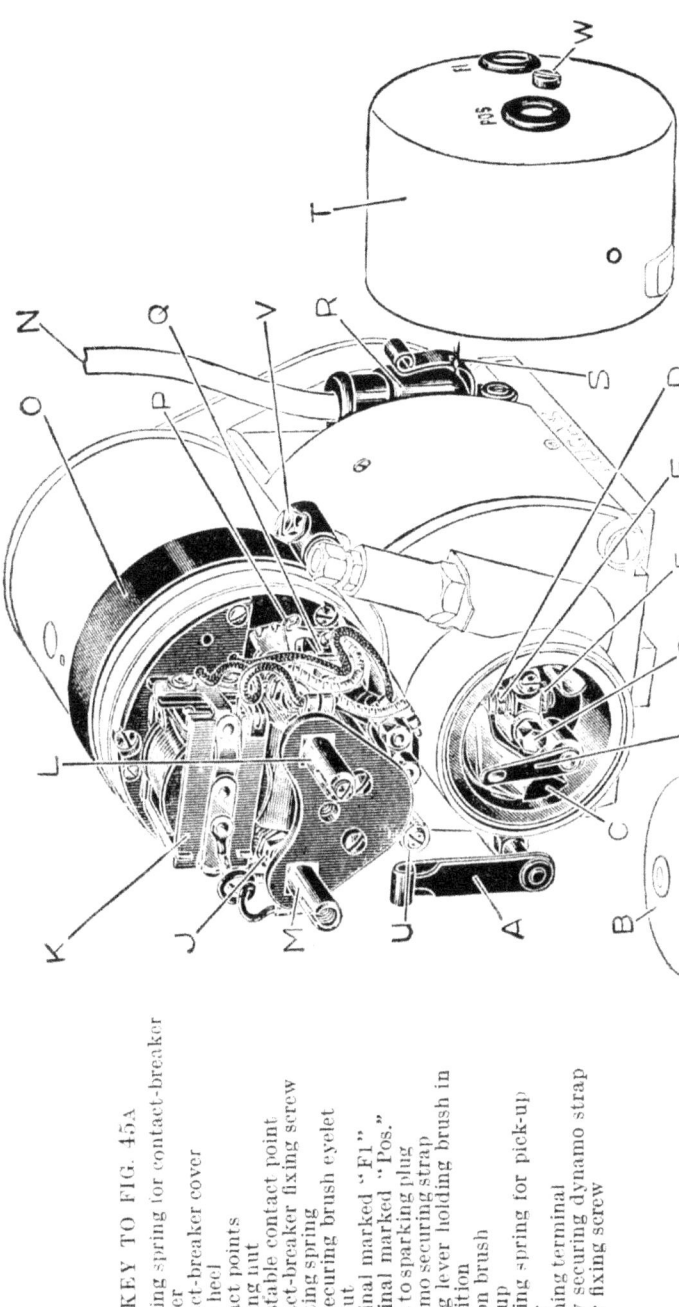

KEY TO FIG. 45A.

A = Securing spring for contact-breaker cover
B = Contact-breaker cover
C = Fibre heel
D = Contact points
E = Locking nut
F = Adjustable contact point
G = Contact-breaker fixing screw
H = Locating spring
J = Nut securing brush eyelet
K = Cut-out
L = Terminal marked "F1"
M = Terminal marked "Pos."
N = Cable to sparking plug
O = Dynamo securing strap
P = Spring lever holding brush in position
Q = Carbon brush
R = Pick-up
S = Securing spring for pick-up
T = Cover
U = Earthing terminal
V = Screw securing dynamo strap
W = Cover fixing screw

FIG. 45A. THE "MAGDYNO" AS FITTED TO SUNBEAMS WITHOUT AUTOMATIC VOLTAGE CONTROL.
(*Messrs. Joseph Lucas, Ltd.*)

are specially made and will give the best results and the longest life. The brushes should be properly "bedded" to the commutator, and unless the owner feels competent to do this, the dynamo should be taken to one of the maker's very efficient service stations.

Cut-out. The cut-out K (Fig. 45A) which is mounted on the dynamo end bracket is an automatic switch which prevents the discharge of the battery through the dynamo windings when the latter is stationary. The contact points close when the dynamo voltage rises above that of the battery as the engine is speeded up, and open when the speed drops and the voltage falls below that of the battery. The cut-out is not fitted with the object of preventing overcharging as some people appear to think. It is inadvisable to tamper or attempt to adjust the cut-out as this is accurately set before leaving the works.

Commutator. The surface of the commutator upon which the brushes bear should be kept perfectly clean and free from oil. The best way to clean the commutator is, without disconnecting any leads, to remove one of the main brushes from its holder and insert a fine duster. Hold it by means of a suitably shaped piece of wood against the commutator surface, at the same time turning the engine in order to rotate the armature.

Unless the commutator has been neglected for a lengthy period it should not be necessary to clean the surface with fine glass-paper instead of a duster.

Wiring of the Equipment. Before making any alteration to the wiring or removing the switch from the back of the headlamp, disconnect the positive lead at the battery to avoid the possibility of short circuits. All the wires in the lighting system are neatly braided together to form a cable assembly or harness. This method of wiring allows the cables to be removed as a complete assembly when taking the electrical equipment off the machine at any time. Another advantage is that the braiding prevents the cables from being "bared" against the frame, causing a short circuit which will cause serious damage to the battery.

All the cables to the headlamp are taken directly into the switch which can easily be withdrawn from the lamp body when the two fixing screws B (Fig. 48) are removed. Thus it will be seen that removing the headlamp in order to compete in reliability trials, racing, etc., does not necessitate any re-wiring.

The ends of all the cables are identified by means of coloured sleevings. The colour scheme is given herewith.

Dynamo, yellow; dynamo field, green; battery, yellow and black; tail lamp, red and black; earth, purple. Wiring diagrams

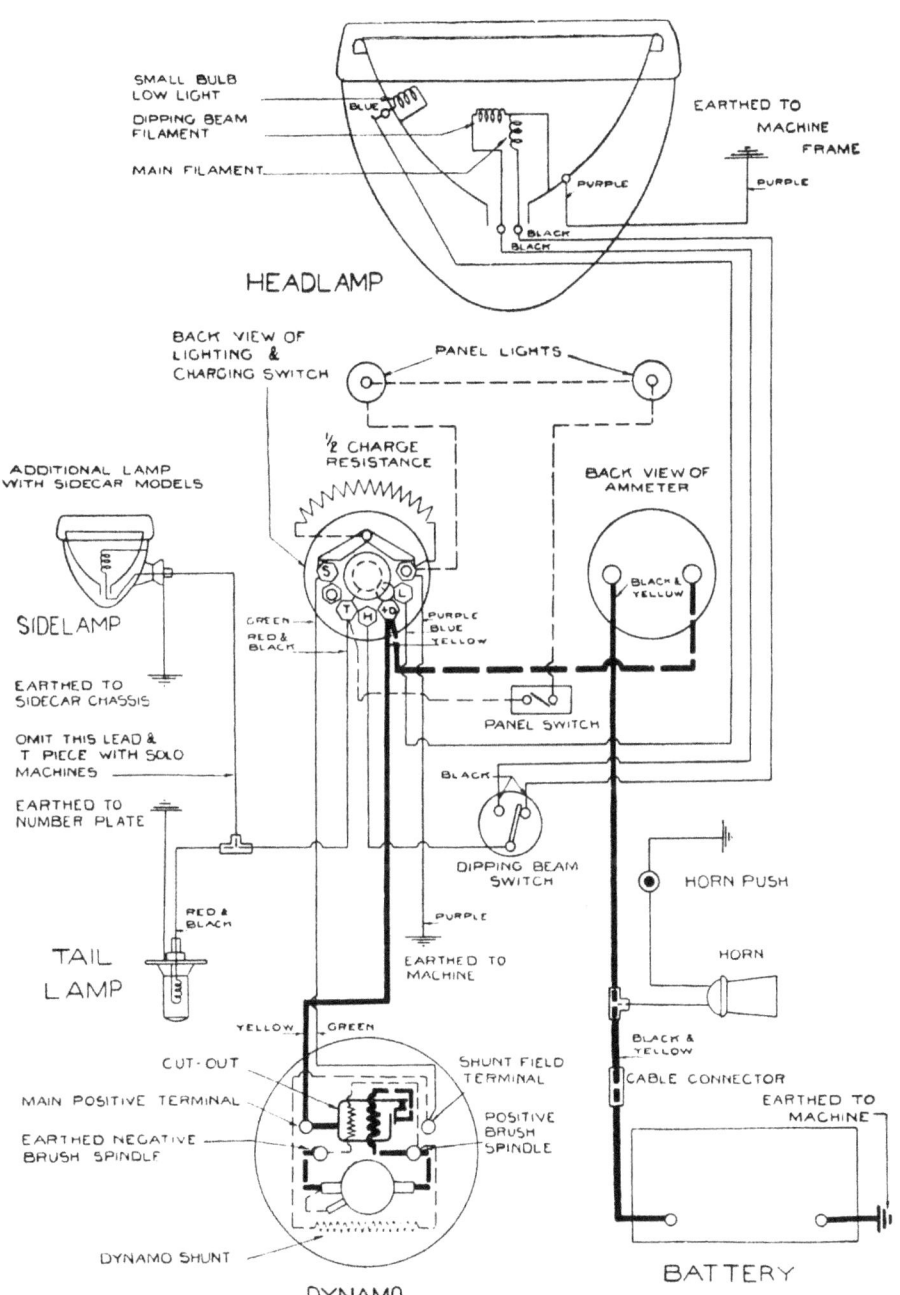

Fig. 45B. Wiring Diagram for Lucas "Magdyno" Lighting System (with Instrument Panel).

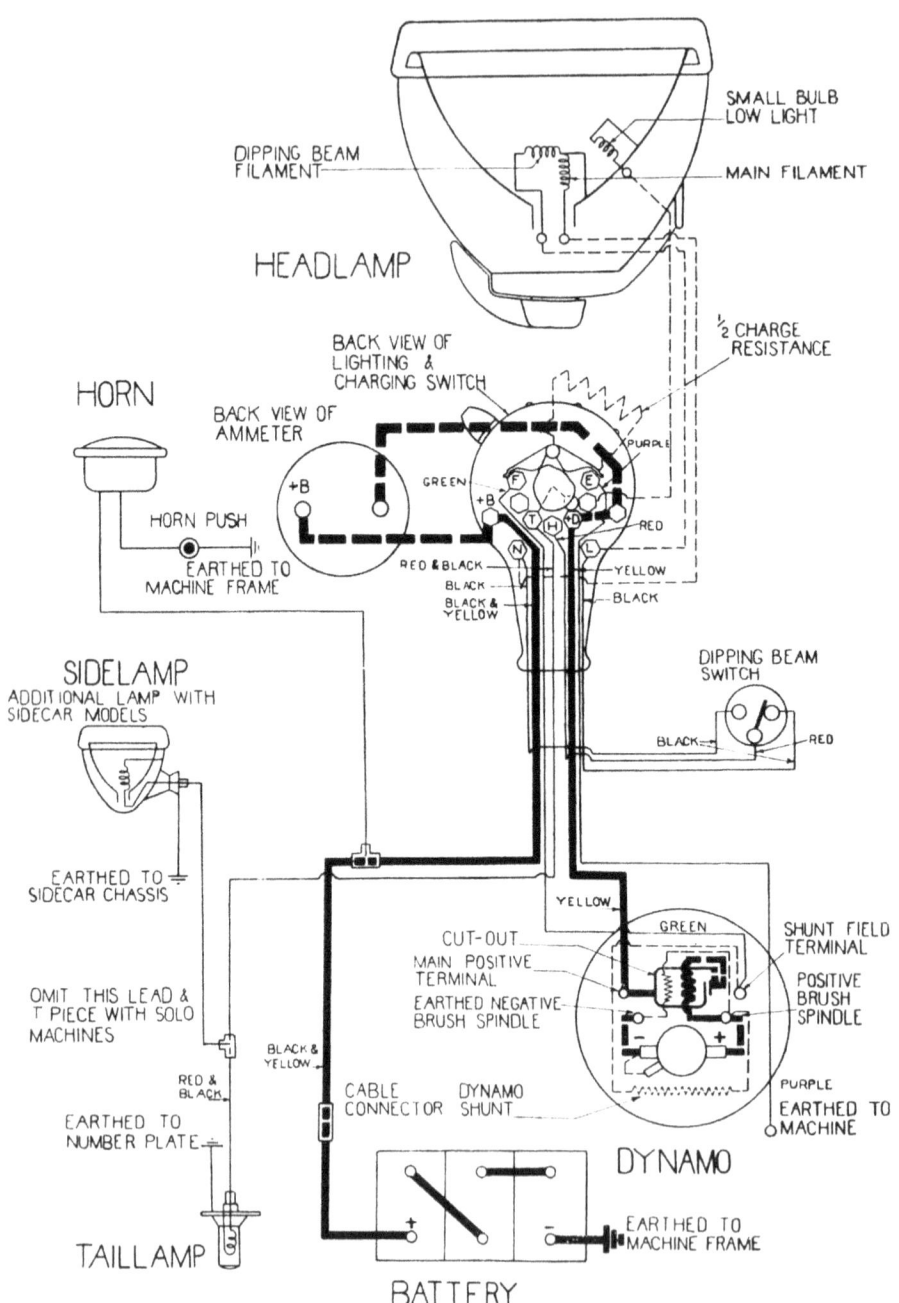

Fig. 45c. Wiring Diagram for Lucas "Magdyno" Lighting System (without Instrument Panel)

ELECTRICAL SYSTEMS

are given in Figs. 45B and 45C. The first one applies only to the Model 90, which, when fitted with electric lighting, has the large 7 in. headlamp and the separate switch on the tank. All the other models are wired up in accordance with the second diagram. A small diagram is situated inside the headlamp and may be seen when the reflector is removed. When making a connection, proceed as follows—

Bare about $\frac{3}{8}$ in. of the cable, twist the wire strands together and turn back about $\frac{1}{8}$ in. so as to form a small ball. Remove

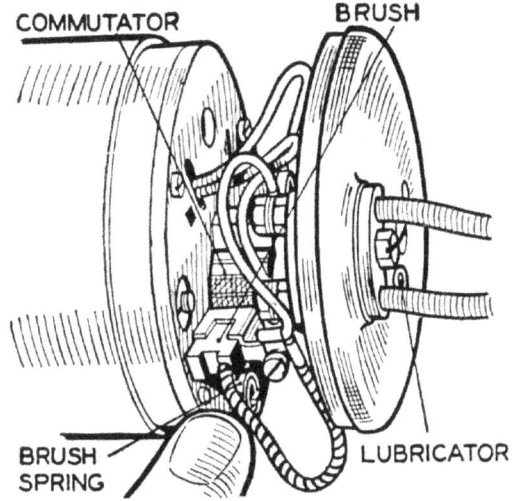

FIG. 46. COMMUTATOR END OF "MAGDYNO" WITH AUTOMATIC VOLTAGE CONTROL

the grub screw from the appropriate terminal and insert the wire so that the ball fits in the terminal part. Now replace and tighten the grub screw. This will compress the ball to make a good electrical connection. The earthing leads from the headlamp and the negative battery terminal must make good electrical contact with the frame as the equipment is wired on the "earth return" system. On the Sunbeam, the battery is earthed by a screw passing through the eyelet on the end of the wire to the front chain case. If this is removed at any time and the earth return terminal moved elsewhere, care must be taken that the enamel round the eyelet is scraped away, otherwise the circuit will not be completed. In the same way it is important to see that the tail lamp makes good contact with the rear number plate, which it will be unable to do if the enamel is not removed as the latter acts as an insulator.

Headlamp (Type H 52). The headlamp is provided with two bulbs, the smaller of which is provided for use when driving in town or when the machine is stationary. The main bulb possesses two filaments, one providing the normal driving light, while the other gives a dipped, anti-dazzling beam for use when meeting traffic or driving in fog or mist. This anti-dazzle is controlled by a switch mounted on the right handlebar. An ammeter is incorporated in the headlamp. This gives an indication that the equipment is working satisfactorily by the needle fluctuating according to whether the current is flowing into, or from the battery. When driving at night, the ammeter is illuminated by indirect lighting.

Switching Arrangement. The central switch (Figs. 47 and 48), which is mounted at the back of the lamp or in the instrument panel, has the following positions—

"Off": Lamps off and dynamo not charging.

"C": Lamps off and dynamo giving half its normal output.

"H": Headlamp (main bulb), tail lamp and sidecar lamp (when fitted) on; dynamo giving maximum output.

"L": With the exception that the pilot bulb is in the place of the main bulb, the conditions are exactly the same as position "H."

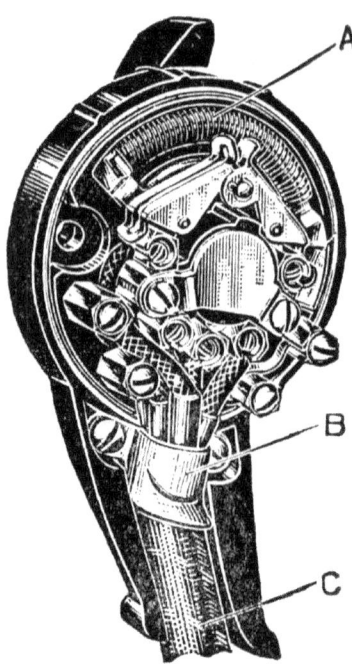

FIG. 47. SWITCH REMOVED FROM BACK OF HEADLAMP

A. Resistance
B. Clamping clip for cables
C. Cable harness

Use of the Charging Switch. The conditions under which motorcycles are used vary considerably, and obviously the amount of charging a battery will require is directly dependent on the extent to which the lamps are used. However, the following suggestions will serve as a rough guide (no A.V.C.).

The switch should be left in the "C" position for about one hour daily. This time should only be increased if the period of night running is considerable, or when the battery is found in a low state of charge (if the specific gravity of the acid solution is 1·210 or below).

The battery must never be left in a fully discharged condition and, unless some long runs are to be undertaken, it is advisable to have the battery removed from the machine and charged up from an independent electrical supply, such as the local wireless

ELECTRICAL SYSTEMS

battery charging station, in the event of the current being completely drained from it.

Removing H52 Headlamp Front and Reflector. To remove the front, hold the edge of the rim with the fingers, press the front evenly with the palm of the hand and then rotate to the left (looking at the front of the lamp).

The reflector is sprung into its position on the three supports (*C* in Fig. 48). When replacing, locate the slot marked "Top" in

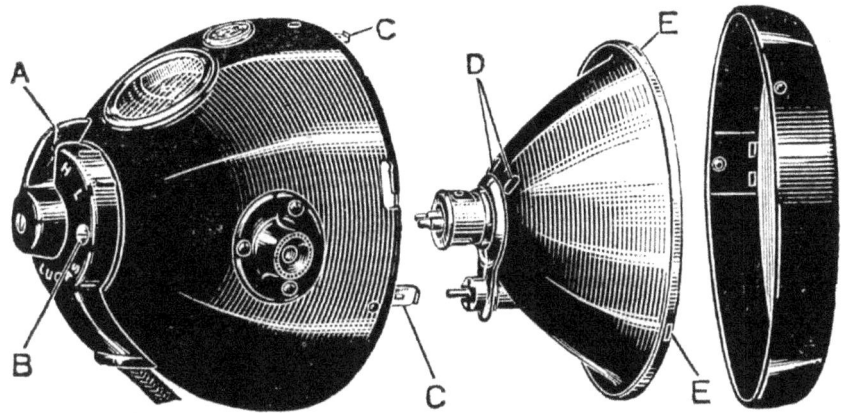

FIG. 48. HEADLAMP TYPE H 52 DISMANTLED

A. Switch
B. Fixing screw
C. Reflector supports
D. Apertures through which light passes to illuminate ammeter
E. Slots in reflector rim

the rear with the top support and then spring the reflector over the other two supports.

Focusing H52 Headlamp. To enable the main bulb filament to be focused correctly, the bulb-holder is arranged so that it can be adjusted. By turning the bulb in a clockwise direction it is moved inwards, and by turning it in an anti-clockwise direction it is moved outwards. The best position can readily be found by trial. When focusing the lamp, it is essential that the road is level and straight. After the correct bulb adjustment has been found, swing the lamp on its pivots until the best road position is obtained. The normal driving light should, of course, be switched on while focusing is being carried out.

Focusing DU Type Headlamps. The best way of focusing and setting the lamp is to take the motor-cycle to a straight, level road, find the correct bulb adjustment, and then move the lamp on its adjustable mounting until the best road position is obtained. On machines with or without an instrument panel the focusing of the headlamp is carried out in the same manner. To focus the main bulb it is necessary to remove the lamp front and reflector by pressing back the fixing clip. Then slacken the clamping screw which secures the bulb-holder and move the bulb-holder and bulb until correct focus is obtained. Afterwards tighten the clamping screw. To remove the bulb-holder it is only necessary to press back the two securing springs. When replacing the lamp front and reflector, the top of the rim should be located first. See that the earthing clip makes good contact with the back of the reflector.

Tail Lamp. The tail lamp, illustrated in Fig. 49, has a ruby glass in the end and a celluloid window at the side, which enables

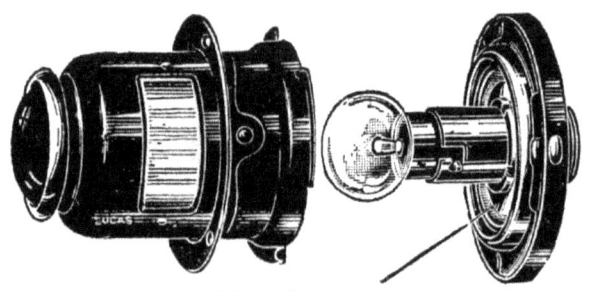

Rubber Diaphragm.
FIG. 49. TAIL LAMP

the bulb to combine the dual functions of illuminating the number plate and showing a red light to the rear. The bulb itself is mounted on a rubber diaphragm which prevents road and engine vibration from being transmitted direct to the filament, thus greatly increasing its life. The rear position of this lamp is removed for a bulb replacement by giving it half a turn to the left when it becomes detached from its fixing.

Cleaning. The lamp reflectors are protected by a transparent and colourless covering which enables any accidental finger-marks to be removed with a soft cloth or chamois leather, without affecting the surface of the reflector. On no account should any metal polishes or other abrasives be used on the reflectors. The ebony black finish of the outer shell can always be restored to its original brilliance with the aid of a good furniture or car polish. Any chromium plated parts only need wiping over with damp cloth to remove dust or dirt.

Replacement Bulbs. When the replacement of any bulb is necessary, it is strongly recommended by the makers that only

Lucas official bulbs are used. The filaments are arranged to be in focus and give the best results with Lucas reflectors. The particulars of replacement bulbs are—

Headlamp (driving and dipped beam lights), No. 70, 24 watts each. Special double filament gas filled bulb.

Headlamp (pilot light), sidecar and tail lamp, No. 200, 3 watts. Centre contact vacuum bulb. Thus it will be seen that in the event of the tail or sidecar lamp "blowing out," the headlamp pilot bulb will satisfactorily interchange. When removing the headlamp main bulb for replacement, screw it out two or three turns in an anti-clockwise direction. Care should be taken that the bulb is fitted the correct way round, i.e. with the dipped beam filament above the centre filament.

Battery Maintenance. If freedom from lighting trouble is to be obtained, it is essential that the battery is maintained in first-class condition. The battery on the Sunbeam is carried in a bracket attached to the oil tank which possesses the two virtues of neatness and freedom from vibration. By far the most important thing is to inspect the battery regularly and keep the acid level $\frac{1}{4}$ in. above the top of the plates by adding distilled water.

Topping Up. At least once a month, the vent plugs in the top of the battery should be removed and the level of the acid solution examined. If necessary, distilled water, which can be obtained at all chemists and most garages, should be added to bring the acid level with the tops of the separators. If, however, acid solution has been spilled, it should be replaced by a diluted sulphuric acid solution of the same specific gravity as in the remaining cells of the battery. When examining the cells do not hold naked lights near vents, as there is a danger of igniting the gas coming from the plates.

Storage. If the equipment is laid by for several months, the battery must be given a small charge from a separate source of electrical energy about once a fortnight, in order to obviate any permanent sulphation of the plates. In no circumstances must the electrolyte be removed from the battery and the plates allowed to dry, as certain chemical changes take place which result in loss of capacity.

Testing Condition of Battery. It is advisable to complete the inspection by measuring the specific gravity of the acid, as this gives a very good indication of the state of charge of the battery. An instrument known as a "hydrometer" is employed for this purpose and should be of the type illustrated in Fig. 50. These can be bought at any of the Lucas service depots.

The specific gravity figures are—
1·280 to 1·300 when fully charged, about 1·210 when half discharged, and below 1·150 when fully discharged. These figures are given, assuming the temperature of the solution is about 60° F.

Take readings of the acid in each cell. The readings should be approximately the same. If one cell gives a reading very different from the rest it may be that the acid has been spilled or has leaked from this particular cell, or there may be a short between the plates. In this case, it is advisable for the owner to have his battery examined by a service depot to trace the cause and prevent the trouble from developing further.

First Filling and Charging of New Batteries. Batteries are sometimes supplied in a dry uncharged condition. The cells should be filled with electrolyte (diluted sulphuric acid) so as to be level with the tops of separators. On pouring the solution into the cells, the specific gravity will gradually fall to the correct Lucas working figure. After filling the battery, give a charge of 2·5 amp. for a period of twelve hours. It will then be fully charged and ready for immediate use. Subsequent charging should be at the rate of 2·5 amp. for six hours.

Automatic Voltage Control. The current "Magdyno" models are fitted with an automatic regulator for the dynamo output, and this is known as the voltage-control unit. It will be found incorporated with the cut-out under the saddle. The object of this device is to keep the battery in a properly charged condition automatically under widely varying conditions. The switch has no "C" position. With this regulator it is possible to use the machine with the battery disconnected and not cause harm.

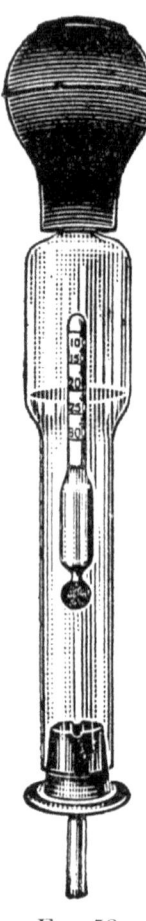

FIG. 50
LUCAS
HYDROMETER

HINTS FOR THE DETECTION AND REMEDY OF FAULTS

Although every precaution is taken to eliminate all possible causes of trouble, failure may occasionally develop through lack of attention to the equipment or damage to the wiring. The most probable faults are tabulated, according to the symptoms which are displayed in the fault-finding tables given opposite.

A few hints are given on the best way to make use of

HOW TO LOCATE AND REMEDY TROUBLE

Table No. 1 (Lighting)

CONDITION	POSSIBLE CAUSES AND METHODS OF DETECTION	REMEDY
Lamps give dim, flickering, or no light when the engine is not running	Bulb filament broken.	Replace with new bulb.
	Bulb discoloured with use.	Replace with new bulb.
	Bulb out of focus.	Focus the bulb until the best illumination is obtained.
	Dirty reflector or bulb.	Clean dirty reflector with chamois leather or a soft cloth.
	Severed or worn cable, or loose connections at headlamp switch, dynamo, or battery.	Tighten loose connections and replace faulty cables.
	Faulty earthing of headlamp. The cable from switch terminal "E" must be securely connected to the earthing terminal on "Magdyno."	Tighten loose connections and replace faulty cables.
	Faulty earthing of battery. The cable from the negative battery terminal must be securely connected to a metal part of the machine.	Tighten loose connections and replace faulty cables.
	Battery exhausted. Take hydrometer readings when acid level is correct ($\frac{1}{4}$ in. above plates) and after a run when electrolyte is thoroughly mixed. When half discharged, readings are about 1·210. When fully discharged, readings are about 1·150.	Machine should be taken on the road for a long daytime run with switch in "C" position or battery charged from independent electrical supply.

HOW TO LOCATE AND REMEDY TROUBLE

Table No. 2 (Lighting)

CONDITION	POSSIBLE CAUSES AND METHODS OF DETECTION	REMEDY
After carrying out examination on Table I, and lamps still give dim, flickering, or no light when the engine is running.	Dynamo not charging, or charging intermittently. Ammeter should give a reading on the charge side when the machine is running at, say, 20 m.p.h. with switch in "C" position. Possible causes of dynamo trouble are—	
	Loose connections at headlamp switch, dynamo or battery.	Tighten loose connections.
	Faulty contacts in headlamp switch.	Examine spring triggers and see that they make good contact with terminals.
	Worn or dirty brushes.	Clean dirty or greasy brushes with a cloth moistened with petrol. Badly worn brushes must be replaced.
	Dirty commutator.	To clean dirty commutator, remove one of the main brushes from its holder and insert a fine duster, holding it pressed against the commutator surface by means of a suitably shaped piece of wood, at the same time slowly turning the engine. If commutator has been badly neglected, clean with very fine glass paper.
	Reversed polarity of dynamo.	To correct polarity of machine, run engine slowly, put switch in "C" position, and then press cut-out contacts momentarily together.

HOW TO LOCATE AND REMEDY TROUBLE

TABLE No. 3 (IGNITION)

CONDITION	POSSIBLE CAUSES AND METHODS OF DETECTION	REMEDY
Engine will not fire or fires erratically.	Remove plug and allow to rest on cylinder head. If a spark occurs at plug points when engine is slowly turned over, the ignition equipment is O.K.	Look for engine defects and check ignition timing.
	If no spark occurs at plug points, remove lead and plug, replace with new length of cable and test independently of plug by holding cable end about $\frac{1}{8}$ in. from metal part of engine. If magneto sparks, H.T. lead of plug is faulty.	Replace H.T. cable if perished or cracked. Clean plug electrodes, adjust gap to about 20 thousandths of an inch.
	If magneto does not spark, possible cause of trouble is:— Contact breaker gap out of adjustment and contacts dirty.	Clean dirty or pitted contacts with fine emery cloth and afterwards with a cloth moistened with petrol. To adjust gap, turn engine slowly until the points are seen to be fully opened, then slacken locking nut and rotate fixed contact screw by its hexagon head until the gap is set to thickness of gauge. After the adjustment, tighten locking nut.
	Contact breaker rocker-arm sticking.	Remove contact breaker and prise rocker-arm off its bearing. Clean steel pin if necessary with fine emery cloth and then, having removed all grit, moisten with a few drops of oil before replacing the lever.
	Pick-up brush worn or broken.	Fit new brush. Before fitting, clean slip ring track.

these tables, as the sources of many troubles are by no means obvious.

Much evidence can be gained from observation of the ammeter. If, for instance, no reading is indicated, when the engine is running at, say, 20 miles per hour with the switch in the "C" position, the dynamo is failing to charge. To ensure that the ammeter is not at fault, the engine should be stopped and the switch turned to "H" position, when a reading on the discharge side of the

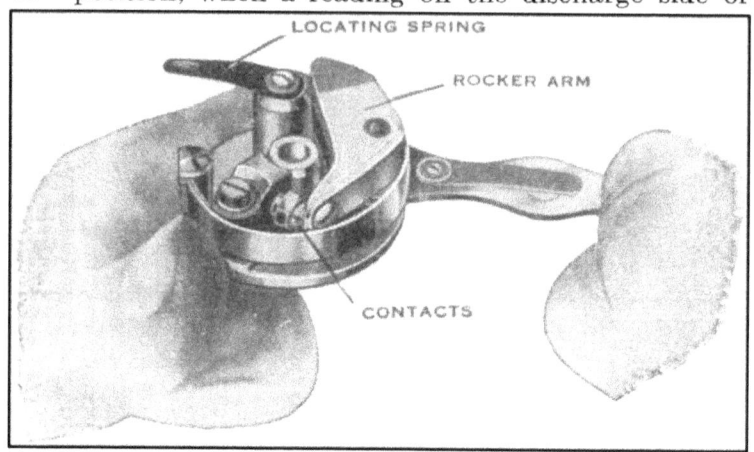

FIG. 51. REMOVING ROCKER ARM FOR CLEANING CONTACTS

scale should be observed. Again, if the needle fluctuates, when the engine is running steadily, an intermittent dynamo output can be suspected. The dynamo may have been neglected and the trouble could be caused by, say, worn brushes or a dirty commutator.

All connections on the equipment should be examined as follows. Remove the switch from the headlamp after disconnecting the positive battery lead. See that all terminals on the switch are tight, move the switch through its four positions, and see that the spring triggers make good contact with the terminals. It sometimes happens that one of the leads fouls the trigger or a portion of the insulation gets clipped between the terminal and the contact. Slight re-arrangement of the wire or cutting back the insulation a fraction will remedy this.

See that the leads to the two moulded terminals on the "Magdyno" are tight, and also that the earthing lead from the headlamp is secured to the terminal at the side of the contact breaker housing.

Finally, re-connect the battery positive terminal and see that the end of the cable from the negative terminal makes good contact with the frame.

ELECTRICAL SYSTEMS

A possible cause of the dynamo failing to charge is the reversal of its polarity due either to the headlamp being ineffectively earthed or to the accidental "shorting" of a terminal or "live" part of the cut-out, when the cover is removed, without the precaution being taken of disconnecting the positive battery lead.

Having examined all the cable connections, the polarity of the dynamo can be corrected by running the engine slowly, putting the switch in the "C" position, and then pressing the cut-out contacts momentarily together when the dynamo should begin to generate again.

MAINTENANCE OF THE MAGNETO

The magneto portion of the "Magdyno" requires very little attention to ensure it gives its best service.

Cleaning. Occasionally examine the contact breaker; the contacts (Fig. 51) must be kept clean and free from all traces of oil.

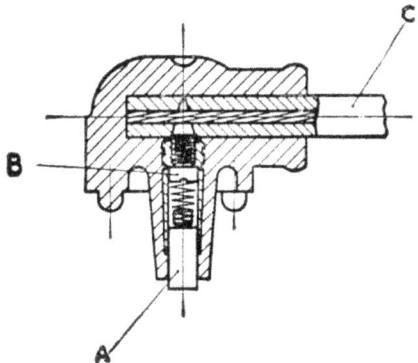

Fig. 52. Method of Securing Cable to Pick-up

If the contacts are burned or blackened, they may be cleaned as follows. Withdraw the contact breaker from its housing by unscrewing the hexagon-headed screw G (Fig. 45A) by means of the magneto spanner. The whole contact breaker can then be pulled off the tapered shaft on which it fits. Now push aside the locating spring H, and prise the rocker-arm off its bearings, when it will be possible to begin cleaning the contacts. Polish them with very fine emery cloth, and afterwards wipe with a cloth moistened with petrol. Care must be taken that all particles of dirt and metal dust are wiped away. Present models have face cam contact breaker.

When replacing the contact breaker, care should be taken to ensure that the projecting key on the tapered portion of the contact breaker base engages with the key-way cut in the armature spindle, or the whole timing of the magneto will be upset. The hexagon-headed screw should be tightened up with care; it must not be too slack, nor must undue force be used.

Next remove the pick-up *R*, and wipe the moulding clean with

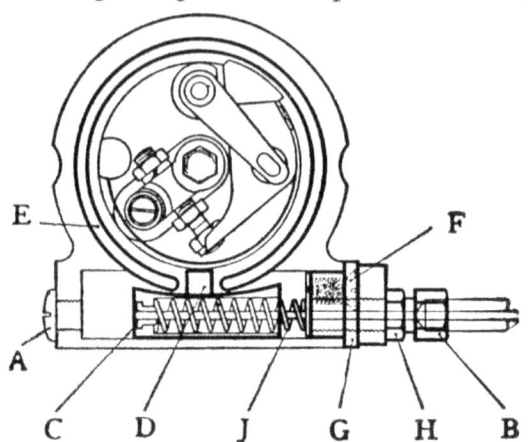

FIG. 53. SECTION OF SPRING CONTROL

A. Screw
B. Cable stop
C. Brass nipple
D. Plunger
E. Cam ring

F. End plate fixing screw
G. End plate
H. Lock nut
J. Spring

a dry cloth. See that the carbon brush moves freely in its holder, being careful not to stretch the brush spring unduly.

Fitting of High Tension Cable. The method of removing the pick-up is illustrated in Fig. 52. Use 7-in. cable and on no account attempt to use a thicker cable pared down to fit. Cut the cable flush to the required length, then remove the pick-up. From the latter withdraw the carbon brush *A*. Slacken the pointed screw *B* and push the cable *C* hard home. Secure by tightening the screw *B* which will pierce the insulation and make good contact with the cable core.

Fitting Bowden Cable to Lucas Magneto Spring Control. Remove the screw *A* (Fig. 53) then, without dismantling any part of the control, thread the Bowden cable through the cable stop *B*. Pass it through the control until it emerges at the hole left by the screw *A*. Now solder the brass nipple *C* to the end of the cable, and then pull it from the other end until it is felt that the nipple fits into the end of the main body of the plunger *D*, when the screw *A* should be replaced.

By referring to Fig. 53, it will be seen that on applying a

ELECTRICAL SYSTEMS

tension to the Bowden cable, the plunger D will move the cam ring E, and so alter the timing of the magneto.

Instructions cannot be given for fitting the cable to the ignition control lever, as the types of these vary. It should be noted, however, that the cable stop B can be adjusted, if necessary to take up any slight slackness of cable covering between the magneto and the lever control.

Should it become necessary at any time to dismantle the spring control and Bowden cable, proceed as follows.

First remove the metal cover of the contact breaker, which is held in position by a spring arm, and then withdraw the cam ring E. Next unscrew the fixing screw F, which is sunk flush with the surface of the end plate G. Then pull the Bowden cable and this will come out, together with cable stop B (which screws into the end plate), lock-nut H, end plate G, and plunger D.

These operations should, of course, be reversed when assembling.

Suitable K.L.G. Sparking Plugs. On page 76 the correct types of Lodge plugs for Sunbeam models are specified. If it is desired to fit a K.L.G. make of plug, it should be noted that the types corresponding to the Lodge H1, H14, and C14 are the K.L.G. M60, F70, and F50 respectively.

Weatherproof Terminals and Plugs. If you are an all-weather rider, it is a good plan to fit a weatherproof terminal to your plug, or alternatively fit a watertight plug. A sectional view of the Lodge weatherproof terminal is shown in Fig. 57. The terminal is shock-proof, weatherproof, and quickly detachable. A K.L.G. type weatherproof terminal which clips on to the K.L.G. plug and completely covers the top insulation is also obtainable.

If fitting a new K.L.G. sparking plug, note that a range of detachable watertight plugs is available. Each plug is obtainable with 18 or 14 mm. thread to suit most engines. The type number of a watertight K.L.G. plug can be identified by the prefix "W." Examples are the WM60, WF70, and WF50.

CHAPTER VII

COMPETITIONS AND COMPETITION WORK

THE Sunbeam has always been right in the forefront in competitions, both on road and track, and its successes abroad have done much to uphold the prestige of British motor-cycles. In the annual Tourist Trophy races held in the Isle of Man, the Sunbeam has an excellent record. It is the opinion of some people that road racing does nothing to improve the ordinary motor-cycle, but there can be no doubt that the T.T. course provides the manufacturers with the finest testing ground possible. The Isle of Man course provides all the varying conditions met with in an ordinary day's run. A glance at the map, Fig. 54, will show that it contains many curves (some gentle and some abrupt); many corners of varying degrees of severity; a steep downhill hair pin at Governor's Bridge; almost as steep an uphill hairpin at Ramsey and corners approached at extremely high speeds such as Creg-na-Baa and Ballacraine. Creg Willeys is a sharp steep hill, as stiff as any main road ascent. The mountain road up Snaefell is a full three miles of really severe climbing, most of it entailing middle gear with long stretches employing low. The corresponding drop down Hillberry is the sort of going where the average rider would "gang warily" unless he had remarkable confidence in his brakes. Last, but not least, there is Sulby Straight, where the machines can be ridden "flat out." The average ordinary solo rider does not get round this difficult 38 miles much under an hour and a half. Moreover the T.T. races consist of seven laps of this course—a total distance of 264 miles. It will be quickly realized, therefore, that speed alone cannot win a T.T. race. For a machine to have a reasonable hope of success it must be extremely good in every respect. It must be as steady as a rock at all speeds. It must be capable of being banked over on bends at amazing angles without skidding. The engine must stand up to merciless thrashing at "all out" speeds without cracking up. All its adjustments must be maintained throughout the period of the race and this is equivalent to a good many thousand miles of ordinary running. The brakes must be enormously powerful in order that the rider can hold his speed until the last possible moment, before having to slow for a corner for it is every second that counts. This entails enormous stresses throughout the machine—tyres, rims, spokes, forks, frame, gear-box, chains, etc., all taking their part as well as the actual brake drums and linings. It will be appreciated at once that any faulty parts would be bound to crack up in this searching test and that these are the exact qualities required by the ordinary rider, only to a lesser degree. The next thing to be recognized, is that in order to go round the Isle of Man course it is necessary to improve the machines in all their qualities, not merely in speed alone. Extra speed is of no use if the machine

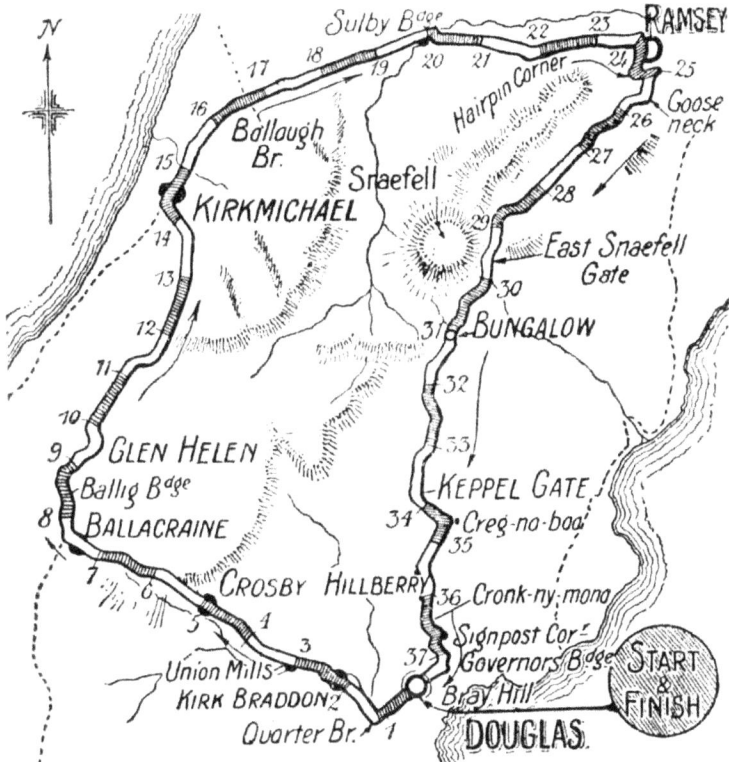

FIG. 54. THE T.T. COURSE IN THE ISLE OF MAN

cannot be steered at the increased speed or if it loses its adjustments more rapidly or if the brakes are not correspondingly better. It is therefore brought about that in order to travel faster round the T.T. course, a machine must be better *all round*, the natural corollary of which is that the best all-round machine is that which can go round the T.T. course the quickest.

It will be understood, therefore, that to be successful in these races, the machines must be as nearly perfect as possible, and why the makers of the Sunbeam have every reason to be proud of their past successes. The Senior T.T. race, the blue riband of motor-cycling has been won by them on no less than four occasions. Four times have they also won the Senior T.T. Team prize—even harder to win than the race itself. Before the start of any T.T. race in the Isle of Man, a manufacturer may nominate three riders of his machine to constitute a team. The fastest team of which all three riders finish, wins the team prize. As a matter of fact, due to the enormous stresses put on the machines, it is very rarely that a team finishes at all. In the Senior T.T. race a nominated team has finished complete on only six occasions, and it is most decidedly a feather in the cap of the makers of the Sunbeam that it has been a Sunbeam which has won the prize on no less than four out of the six occasions, namely, in 1914, 1923, 1928, and 1929. This achievement testifies to the unfailing reliability which is to be found in every Sunbeam motor-cycle.

Abroad, the Sunbeam has won practically every one of the premier Continental road races. In 1929, for example, they succeeded in winning the French Grand Prix at an average speed of 76 m.p.h.; the Belgian Grand Prix; the Austrian Grand Prix; the Hungarian Grand Prix; the Grand Prix of Nations; and the Italian Senior T.T. Race. A very formidable list of successes for one year's racing.

Reliability Trials. Besides the innumerable racing successes, the makers of the Sunbeam have been extraordinarily successful in reliability events. Reliability trials provide a searching test for the machines in all types of colonial going, including rocky hills, long mud sections and water-splashes. It is therefore interesting to relate that in 1929, for example, the Premier Award in the Colmore, Victory, and Reliance Trials was in each case won by a Sunbeam private owner, Mr. N. P. O. Bradley. He was also successful in making the best performance in the Kickham Memorial Trial and the Southern Trial. All these successes gained in the one year on the same machine prove the unfailing reliability of the Sunbeam. Three other events of a somewhat different character—the Scott Trial, the Ilkley Grand National, and the Lancashire Grand National were all won by Mr. V. N. Brittain riding a Model 9. These rough-riding events or cross country scrambles are held generally over wild moorland country with innumerable obstacles, and provide a searching test for both man and machine.

Besides the above, which of course are the most important events, there are countless awards won practically every week during the season by Sunbeam riders, mostly with the everyday ride-to-work machines. This emphatically demonstrates the fact that the sporting rider will find a Sunbeam eminently suitable for business purposes, while the utility rider, should the fancy take him, can perform with success in the various competitive events.

Competition Riding. Although the author realizes that not every Sunbeam owner is interested in competition work, it is proposed for the benefit of those who wish to display their prowess and the many virtues of their machines, to give a few hints on preparing the machines.

There are many types of competitions, among which may be numbered reliability trials, road racing, grass track racing, scrambles (ultra sporting trials), and freak hill climbs. As in practically all these speed is really an essential, the most suitable machines are the overhead valve models, that is, Models 10, 9, 90. The owner of a side valve model would find it perfectly suitable for ordinary trials work, but would no doubt find himself outclassed in an acceleration test. As acceleration tests are frequently used to determine the Premier Award, it is advisable for the keen clubman to purchase an O.H.V. model if he intends doing a good deal of competition work.

Speed Events. In track and grass track work, the tuning of the engine is of primary importance, although it must be borne in mind that it is a waste of time "super-tuning" the engine if the gear ratios are all wrong or the machine cannot be steered at its maximum. The Model 90 is turned out standard by the manufacturers as capable of round about 90 m.p.h., so it will be realized that this machine can be entered for speed events in practically its standard form.

However, the following may be of assistance in obtaining those few extra "revs" which count so much.

The Piston. As probably the greatest frictional losses occur at the piston, it is essential that the piston be dead free, and free from high spots. After the engine has been carefully run-in, remove the piston and examine for any highly polished patches standing out on the aluminium. These should be very carefully removed with a fine file. The rings must bed nicely in the groves and touch the barrel equally all round. When fitting rings for speed work, the gap should be as shown in Fig. 55, and there should be a clearance of four to five thousandths of an inch in the ring groves. The rings should be well lapped in with metal polish, both on their diameters and sides. The speed of an engine can almost invariably be increased by the fitting of a high compression piston, but as the standard Model 90 is fitted with a $7\frac{1}{2}$ to 1 compression ratio, any advance on this necessitates the use of alcohol fuel. As any one who intends using fuels such as RD 1 or PMS 2, should be well versed in tuning, it is not the author's intention to delve into the realms of "dope."

Valve Gear. Stronger valve springs may be fitted, but these are not recommended for ordinary work as they intend to overload the cam gear. The valve seating should not be too narrow as it is essential that the heat should be carried away as effectively as possible to the cylinder head. Seven sixty-fourths of an inch will be found about right. The timing gear should be absolutely free, the cam levers being dead square with the cam wheel as shown in Fig. 56. Failure to observe this will put excessive

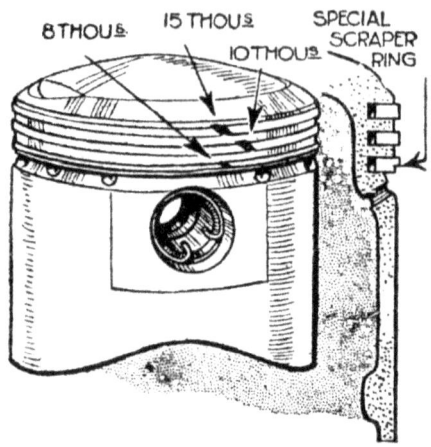

FIG. 55. THE SUNBEAM PISTON, SHOWING THE RING-GAPS, THE GUDGEON-PIN FIXING, AND A SECTION THROUGH THE THREE RINGS
(*From "The Motor Cycle"*)

stresses on the valve operating gear, owing to the thrust of the cam not being evenly distributed, and consequently the cam and its lever will wear badly. Any inaccuracy at this point can be rectified by the judicious use of carborundum stick.

Cylinder Head and Ports. The cylinder head and ports, especially the inlet, should be carefully polished out. These may be done with the aid of riflers, round files, and metal polish. Particular attention should be paid to the inlet port in order that the incoming gas should have a nice smooth passage with as little obstruction as possible.

The Carburettor. The tuning of the carburettor is dealt with elsewhere, but a few words here will not come amiss. The main duty of the carburettor is to provide for as big a volume of gas as may be demanded by the engine, a consideration which is governed by valve timing, port areas, and the nature of the induction passages. Guard against running on a weak mixture as this causes overheating, a fatal condition from all points of view. To find the best jet setting, commence with a rather rich mixture and after running for a time, take out the sparking plug and note its condition. Should the mixture be over-rich, a burnt fuel deposit will be found on the electrodes and the base of the plug. Carry out experiments, using a jet two sizes smaller each time, until the plug is clean. If the mixture is much too weak, the exhaust pipe will show a variety of hues, from deep blue to straw.

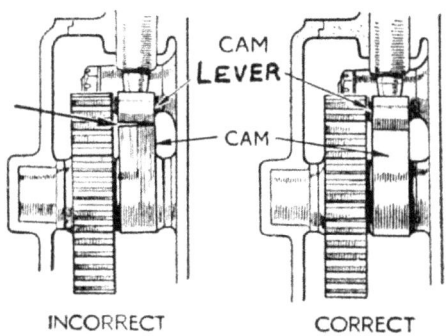

FIG. 56. SHOWING EFFECT OF A BADLY ALIGNED CAM LEVER

In passing, it should be mentioned that chromium-plated exhaust pipes do not discolour in the ordinary way.

Cycle Parts. Good steering is absolutely essential for high speed work and, with this in mind, see that the fork spindles are well greased and free and that no sideplay exists in the links. Probably the best size tyres for all-round work are 27 in. × 2·75 in. front, and 27 in. × 3·00 in. rear. The wheels must be free and dead in line. If they are not already balanced, balance them with split lead shot gripped on the spokes diametrically opposed to the tyre valve. The transmission plays a very important part, inasmuch as friction at this point will knock several m.p.h. off the maximum speed. See that the sprockets are dead in line, and the use of a straight edge will ensure perfect results. The chains should be adjusted as previously mentioned in Chapter II, and it is essential to make sure that they are constantly lubricated, as at high speeds a chain heats up fairly quickly.

Riding Position. For actual track work, the handlebar grips should point directly downwards as this position will be found the least tiring to the fore-arm muscles when a strong grip has to be maintained for a lengthy period. Use the knee-grips and keep the knees and feet glued to the rests, as this will be found to make for steadiness. As at high speeds, the air pressure is tremendous, and therefore quite an important feature is that of reducing wind resistance to the absolute minimum. The rider should endeavour to be practically horizontal so that no portion of the body projects, in order to offer as little wind resistence as possible.

Correct Gearing. Correct gearing is absolutely essential if any degree of success is to be obtained. In speed trials, either a standard clutch start or a short "flying" start are employed so that to all intents and purposes they are acceleration tests. It can be safely said that most riders habitually overgear in the hope of obtaining more speed. This is totally wrong as will be shown by the following. First ascertain the length of the flying start (if used) and test the machine by noting how far it has to travel before the maximum speed is attained. Then lower the gear and try again. With the correct ratio it will be found that the machine will attain its maximum much quicker. For example, say that 90 m.p.h. can be attained on the ordinary ratio and 80 m.p.h. on the lower one, but the maximum on the latter is reached in 400 yards instead of the 700 yards required by the higher gear. It will be seen that the lower gear will be much faster over the half mile with a short flying start. In acceleration tests, avoid as far as possible changing gear as vital seconds may be lost, especially if the gears are "muffed." Practise starting over and over again, as a good start is of paramount importance.

Watch the "cracks" getting away and notice their method of handling throttle and clutch; the most unobtrusive start is almost invariably the fastest.

The above remarks apply in many instances to the next subject, that of trial riding, although each is, in its way, a specialized form of sport.

Trial Riding. The most popular competitive event is undoubtedly the one or half-day reliability trial, and these may be split up into three sections; (a) The Open; (b) The Open to Centre (c) restricted or minor club events. The open trials are generally run by a big club and are mostly supported by the trade. "The Colmore" and "The Victory" are two typical "Open" events. Owing to the great preponderance of trade riders on very carefully prepared machines, it is inadvisable for the novice to enter an "open" event to start his trial riding career.

The "Open to Centre" trials are organized by different clubs in the various centres of the Auto Cycle Union for the benefit of members of any club in that centre. For example, the Sunbeam M.C.C., which is a constituent club of the South Eastern Centre of the A.C.U., will organize a trial open to any club in the South Eastern Centre, an area which extends over Kent, Surrey, Sussex, and Hampshire. Although in centre events, the novice will have practically all amateurs as competitors, he will be opposed to the crack riders from each individual club and it is for this reason that the author would suggest beginning in the "restricted" or "small club events."

When the intending trials rider receives his prospectus, he should study the rules very carefully, paying special attention to any "special tests" which may figure in the regulations. The reason why the trade man so often pulls off the Premier Award is because he has scrutinized the regulations carefully and prepared

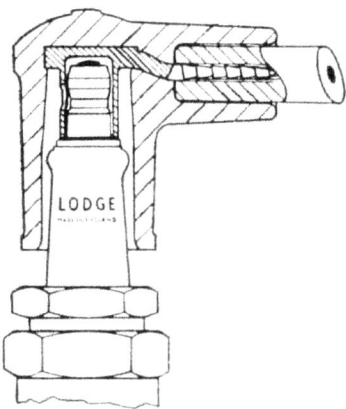

FIG. 57. THE LODGE WEATHERPROOF TERMINAL

his machine accordingly. If the actual route to be employed can be learnt beforehand, it is an advantage to put in a little practising, particularly on the observed hills, although it must be borne in mind that a hill may be altered out of all recognition on the day of the event by a heavy downpour of rain overnight.

As regards the riding in the actual event, it is largely a matter of common sense and the ability to do the right thing at the right moment. For instance, you take a water-splash fast and stop, due to water in the ignition department. The splash is then taken slowly and you get through feet up — therefore splashes should be taken slowly. Perhaps it is necessary to take water fast in certain events, so therefore watch where the splashes go. The front wheel throws water on the plug, so fit a waterproof cover similar to the one shown in Fig. 57. Muddy water is thrown up by the rear wheel on to the sidecar and rebounds into the carburettor — a shield over the carburettor will prove an effective remedy. Occasionally, if really deep water is to be encountered, an extra long air-intake pipe can be made out of a piece of car radiator hose. This should be of larger diameter than the air-intake, otherwise the carburation will be considerably affected and, in any case, it will probably be found necessary to readjust the carburettor. To prevent water getting into the magneto smear the contact breaker cover with plasticine or grease. This should be applied shortly before the event and removed as soon as possible afterwards, as it is very detrimental to the magneto to run it absolutely air-tight for a lengthy period.

As regards riding position and weight distribution, the golden rule is to keep the front of the machine as light as possible and, with this object in view, remove the headlamp if possible, fit a light sports guard and either adjust the handlebars or alter the bend so that as little weight as possible is borne in the front. A pair of "Sit-up-and-beg" handlebars also have the advantage of allowing the rider to place all his weight over the rear wheel, which greatly assists wheel grip. The footrests should be placed fairly low—approximately 9 in. from the ground, and the saddle about 27 in. from the ground.

Tyres. The tyres play a tremendously important part in trial work and, without the special tyres with large "knobs" on the sides, known as the Dunlop "Sports," it is almost impossible to attain any measure of success. The recommended sizes are 27 in. × 2·75 in. front and 26 in. × 3·25 in. solo, while if there is sufficient clearance, a 27 in. × 4·00 in. may be fitted to a sidecar machine, as in the case of the latter, grip is of paramount importance. The object of the small section front tyre is two-fold, firstly, to lighten the steering, and secondly, to enable the machine to be steered out of gullies easily. The tyre pressures are important, and for greasy observed hills the tyres should be deflated until they are quite "flabby." Too hard a tyre pressure causes skids on a solo machine and wheel spin on a combination. A spare wheel is a considerable asset to a combination, and this should preferably be mounted between the back wheel and the sidecar, where it assists wheel grip but does not cause the outfit to "crab" badly. An additional advantage of the spare wheel is that it may be fitted just prior to the attempt on a "super" observed hill, and the extra grip given by the new clean tyre may make all the difference between the Premier Award and a silver medal.

Perhaps a few words on how to treat various types of observed hills and sections will not be amiss. The method of attack can be summarized in the table shown on the opposite page.

It should not be found necessary to use the damper except in scrambles. The fork damper should be "tightish" for rough stuff and fairly loose for tricky bits of grease.

Many of the foremost professional riders stand on the footrests over rough stuff and this is well worth trying as it considerably aids controllability. The only drawback to this practice is that

COMPETITION TABLE

Condition of Surface	Method	Comments
1. Squelchy mud	Fast	Second gear
2. Greasy mud	Slow	Careful
3. Small loose rocks	Fairly fast	None
4. Large loose boulders	Dead slow	Ready with clutch
5. Tight greasy rocks any size	Dead slow	Ready with clutch
6. Sand (all kinds)	Flat out	Second gear with "taps" open
7. Water splashes	Slow	Engine turning over fairly fast, clutch partly disengaged

it savours of the keeping of all the eggs in one basket, inasmuch as if the model takes charge the rider is bound to come "unstuck."

It will be realized that the above tips apply mainly to a solo machine, although some are, of course, applicable to a combination.

The tips given next are for the benefit of the sidecar trials aspirant.

Get in plenty of practice. Practise, particularly, keeping to the right up greasy hills, so that there is time to correct crabbing; practise opening out on good bits of surface and shutting off on bad; practise taking hairpins wide, cutting across them invariably courts disaster. Cultivate the "feel" of the throttle in order that wheel-spin may be prevented and finally get in plenty of practice for special tests.

Eliminate all articles which tend to stop progress, i.e. if a footrest or exhaust pipe catches, raise it. (Incidentally, the makers supply high clearance exhaust pipes for trials work at no extra charge.) If the crankcase fouls on rocks, fit a steel undershield; if the front mudguard clogs, bend the end in so that it almost touches the tyre and acts as a scraper.

Carry a good kit of tools accessibly disposed, a spare clutch wire, and a spare clean plug.

Finally, the author earnestly recommends that the rider should attend the big open trials to watch the successful riders in action, individual riding varies, but the rider is almost sure to find one on whom he can model his style.

CHAPTER VIII

OVERHAULING

Valve Spring Removal. As no doubt the reader will have seen, pages 37 and 38 deal effectively with the tools and methods necessary for the removal of the valve springs, but for the benefit of the reader who has not the special tools, supplied by the makers, available, the tools depicted in Figs. 58 and 59 are quite easily made up. Fig. 58 shows a hairpin valve spring compressor, which consists of a long coach bolt, a distance piece, a piece of steel plate, and wing nut. Cut from the steel plate a piece about $1\frac{3}{4}$ in. × $1\frac{1}{2}$ in., and in the middle cut a square to take the square of the coach bolt. Bend the outer edges upwards as shown in sketch. The piece of steel underneath the bush should be drilled $\frac{5}{16}$ in. and bent to shape as depicted. The last operation is to grind the head of the coach bolt flat. This handy little tool once made will be found to be invaluable when decarbonizing.

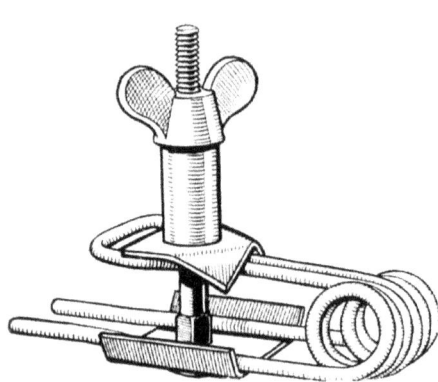

FIG. 58. THE HAIRPIN VALVE SPRING COMPRESSOR IN ACTION
(*From "The Motor Cycle"*)

Valve Guides. After the machine has been decarbonized several times the reader, while engaged on grinding-in the valves, will discover, no doubt, that wear has taken place between the valve guides and stem. The major portion of wear will be found to have taken place on the valve guide, and this should be renewed, otherwise the slow running and starting will be impaired, owing to the leakage of air affecting the carburation. Valve guide removal is comparatively simple provided it is gone about in the right way. Obtain first a bolt long enough to take a distance piece slightly longer than the valve guide together with a large washer and nut. The bolt head should be able to pass through the valve guide housing. Pass the bolt through the guide from the port end; the distance piece should then be placed over the bolt to surround the valve guide flange. Next the large washer and finally the nut. By tightening the nut and holding the bolt at the same time, the valve guide will be extracted. This only applies to the side valve and O.H. coil spring type of guides. For the hairpin type valve guide a piece of steel strip made up in a "U" formation to fit across the base of the guide, with a hole in the centre, should be substituted for the distance piece. When refitting the new guides a large washer should be substituted for the distance tube, the procedure being similar to that for the

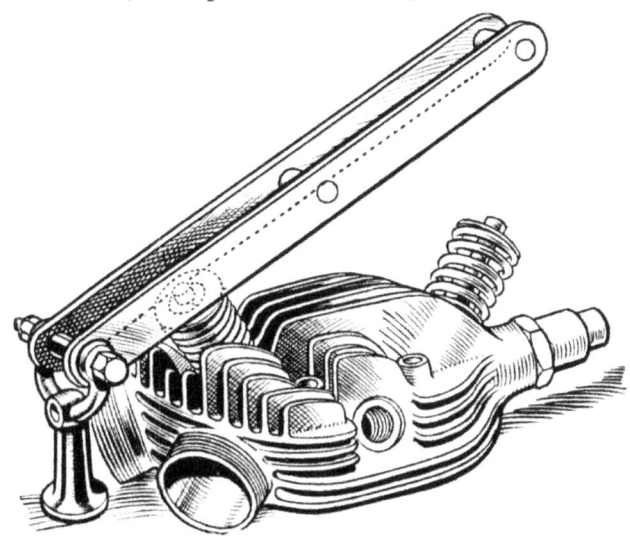

FIG. 59. THE OVERHEAD VALVE SPRING REMOVING TOOL IN USE
(*From "The Motor Cycle"*)

removal. Always make sure that the valve guide housing is carefully washed out with petrol before the new guide is inserted. A somewhat crude method of removal is with a hammer and punch, but with this method there is every possibility of fracturing the guide, apart from the chance that the guide may be fitted out of truth. A distorted valve guide has a very deleterious effect on the valve, wearing the stem rapidly on one side and tending to hammer the valve seat. Should play still be in evidence after new guides have been fitted, then it will be necessary to replace the valves. With the patent Sunbeam lubrication system which ensures a copious supply of lubricant at the valve guides, renewal of the guides is only necessary at infrequent intervals.

Valve Grinding. Whilst still on the subject of valves there is one important aspect of valve grinding not dealt with on pages 38 and 39, that which affects badly pitted valve seats. Many motor-cyclists make the mistake of grinding away until all the deep pits are removed, and in the process remove nearly all the valve seat. This has the evil effect of lowering the valve lift, and the lack of metal at the seat prevents the dissipation of heat, causing overheating and loss of power. In the case of badly pitted seats the head should be turned over to a garage who will be able to reface the seats with a special cutter. The valve seats themselves may be faced up in a lathe to prevent unnecessary grinding. Alternatively, the works will be pleased to undertake the work for a small charge.

Decarbonizing. An alternative method of decarbonizing a longstroke cylinder barrel to that mentioned on page 35 is that of laying the barrel in a solution of caustic soda and water mixed in a preparation of 3 lb. of caustic to 1 gal. of water. The cylinder should be left in the solution for approximately 2 hours, when the carbon will be found to have dissolved. Finish off by washing the barrel in warm water to remove any traces of the caustic. *On no account should the* 1935 *light alloy heads be treated by this method or any other article apart from cast iron.*

Clutch Slip. The following will be of assistance in the event of the rider experiencing clutch slip, the symptoms of which are considerable "revving" of the engine with a reduced road speed and difficulty in climbing hills. The first operation is to check whether the inner cable is stranded, which would prevent the clutch from engaging. On the 95 Models the clutch withdrawal is operated by a quick-pitch thread in the gear-box bridge with a knurled finger adjuster. The adjustment is correct when the clutch lever on the handlebar is just free without any excessive movement. If there is not enough freedom of movement, the clutch plates will be held out of engagement, causing the clutch to slip. Should the cable have stretched, which will be indicated by excessive movement and difficulty in changing gear, due to the clutch plates not disengaging correctly, the adjustment can be taken up by the knurled cable adjuster. Pages 61 and 62 deal with the adjustment on the other models except the 250 c.c., the adjustment of which is obvious.

Clutch Corks. Undue "revving" of the engine with the clutch partially disengaged will cause the clutch corks to wear or burn out, with inevitable slipping of the clutch. It is recommended that the clutch plates should be returned to the works, who will supply a set of service plates by return of post at a small cost. In an emergency, medicine bottle corks glued with fish glue or seccotine and carefully cut with a razor blade, can be used, but great care should be taken to cut the corks to a uniform level.

1937 MODELS

Attention to Gear-box. With the careful selection of material and the high standard of workmanship insisted upon by the makers, trouble in the gear-box may be regarded as practically negligible. If a fault should develop in the box, it is advisable to return it to the makers for attention. Where the rider has the necessary skill and the desire to rectify any defect himself attention should be given to the following points. The outer cover together with the nuts round the kick-starter case cover should be removed and the mainshaft nut and the small nuts holding the case in position unscrewed after which the gears will be exposed. It is not necessary to dismantle the kick-starter. The gear assembly may be removed from the shell *en bloc* by releasing the pawl spring. When reassembling care should be taken when fitting the camshaft rollers and sector mechanism. Thick grease should be used to keep the rollers in position when the kick-starter case may be refitted with ease. Correct location of the gears is ensured by marking the small gear on the end of the camshaft and the gear sector with the letter "O." The markings should coincide when the gears are assembled correctly. The gears are all of the constant mesh variety and control is obtained by a camshaft fitted with Alum-bronze operating forks and mounted on roller bearings. In place of the five dogs previously fitted the actual gear teeth are now extended and engage with internal teeth cut on the face of the adjoining gears, ensuring the minimum of backlash.

Foot Gear Change. To obtain access to the foot gear change, unscrew the six nuts round the cover when the mechanism will be exposed to view. The gear changes are effected by a double-edged pawl engaging with a ratchet. A specially constructed aluminium box loaded with springs controls the amount of movement ensuring that the gears are not missed and that the operating lever is brought back to the same position after each gear change.

When reassembling, the sector should be refitted first, engaging with the gear on the end of the camshaft, taking care that the letter "O" stamped on both sector and camshaft coincide. Part of the control is already in position in the kick-starter case cover and with the assistance of some thick grease the pawl may be affixed to the quadrant immediately facing the ratchet. The kick-starter case cover may then be fitted to the gearbox. The foot change control should then be tested by hand.

Gear-box Lubrication. The gear-box is fully charged with grease when leaving the works and will probably leak slightly until the correct level is reached. The level should be checked up frequently and it may be necessary to add 2-3 oz. of grease every 1000 to 1200 miles. The recommended lubricants are Wakefield's Castrolease Medium, Vacuum Mobilgrease No. 2, or Shell Motor Grease (Soft). After extensive tests the makers have found that these light greases effectively lubricate the wearing parts without the viscosity being lowered to the same extent as gear oil and actually result in smaller friction losses.

Clutch Adjustment. When wear takes place in the clutch friction surfaces resulting in the handlebar control lever tightening up, the clutch cable should be detached from the operating lever and adjusted by means of the screw situated behind the operating lever. It is imperative that there should not be less than $\frac{1}{16}$ in. play in the lever. The adjusting screw regulates a ball incorporated in the loose sleeve in the mainshaft and should it be necessary to remove the sleeve take note that the ball is not lost.

Front Chain Adjustment (250 c.c., 350 c.c. and 500 c.c. Light Solo Models). Remove the chain-case inspection cap and loosen the two stud nuts. The gear-box pivots on the long stud passing through the lug at the bottom of the gear-box shell. A lug on the upper side of the gear-box casing registers with two stays having slots, and the second stud passes through both the stays and the lug. Move the gear-box in the required direction until there is about $\frac{1}{2}$ in. movement in the middle when the chain is at its tightest. It is advisable to re-check the adjustment after the nuts securing the gear-box have been retightened.

Front Chain Adjustment (Model 9 and Lion). On these models the bolt which secures the top lug of the gear-box to the frame and the one which passes through the bottom lug and screws into the lug on the chainstay of the frame must be loosened, and the adjuster situated under the gear-box at the rear screwed in or out as required. To tighten screw in a clockwise direction. Allow $\frac{3}{4}$ in. vertical movement for correct adjustment.

Rear Chain Adjustment (All Models). Slacken the wheel spindle nut on the right hand side and the brake sleeve nut on the left-hand side. Next unscrew the right-hand adjustor in the fork end clear of the wheel spindle, and screw the left-hand chain adjustor in until the correct adjustment which should be $\frac{3}{4}$ in. vertical movement is obtained. If the brake sleeve nut is tightened up first followed by the spindle nut and lastly the right-hand chain adjustor, there will be no possibility of the alignment being upset.

Backlash Compensating Cams. The present 500 c.c. and 600 c.c. models are fitted with special cams which are designed to be silent in operation and to eliminate backlash in the timing gear. If it is necessary to disturb the timing, proceed as follows—

Inlet Cam. (1) Hold the cam with the contour in a vertical position and with the back of the gear facing you. The small cam on the adjusting screw should be set as far as possible to the right.

(2) The loose gear with the spring in position should next be fitted to the loose cam and turned in an anti-clockwise direction until the loose movement is lost.

(3) Grip the two gears with the left hand and turn the adjusting screw until the spring locks the screw in position. Half a turn is sufficient for the spring to lock the screw which will be indicated by a slight click. It should be possible on gently easing off the grip to move the loose gear 2 to $2\frac{1}{2}$ teeth backwards.

(4) Once the adjusting screw is set to the original position, no trouble should be experienced in fitting the cam into the timing case.

Exhaust Cam. Follow the instructions given in parts (1) and (2) on the inlet cam and holding the cam firmly turn the loose gear clockwise 2 to $2\frac{1}{2}$ teeth. It will be necessary to insert a metal wedge into the teeth to hold the gear in position when refitting into the timing case. When the cam meshes with the crankshaft pinion the wedge will drop out. Punch marks are provided on the centre pinion and the timing cam and these must be in register for correct valve timing.

Ignition Timing. The ignition timing set out in the table below should be adhered to closely and need only be varied when the engine has been tuned for speed.

250 c.c. O.H.V.	$\frac{11}{16}$ in. before top dead centre
350 c.c. O.H.V.	$\frac{11}{16}$ in. do.
500 c.c. Light Solo Sports	$\frac{11}{16}$ in. do.
500 c.c. Light Solo	$\frac{9}{16}$ in. do.
500 c.c. Model 9	$\frac{9}{16}$ in. do.
600 c.c. Model 9	$\frac{9}{16}$ in. do.

The above settings are correct when the control lever on the handlebars is set at full advance and the contact breaker points just about to separate.

Lubrication of the O.H.V. Gear. The rocker box is fed with oil under pressure and a needle type adjuster is incorporated in the system. This provides that the box will receive the correct amount of oil and the usual setting is between 1½ and 2 complete turns open from the closed position. A locknut is provided on the adjustor and this must be securely tightened after the adjustment has been effected.

Hub Adjustment. The 1937 models are fitted with taper roller bearings in the hubs and these are designed to run for lengthy periods without need of adjustment. To effect the necessary adjustment, place the wheel on the stand and unscrew the left-hand spindle nut. This will permit the locknut inside the fork end to be loosened. The adjusting nut can then be taken up but due allowance must be made for tightening the locknut. It is imperative that a slight shake can be felt in the bearings. Take note that the right-hand spindle nut must not be slackened off when effecting adjustment. In the case of the rear wheel it is necessary to remove this from the frame before adjustment can be made. It should be noted that the sleeve has a slot in the right-hand side which can be utilized whilst the locknut and washer are being removed. Adjustment is carried out in a similar way to that of the front wheel. Once again taking particular care that a slight movement is allowed in the bearing. This method of adjustment is also applicable to the detachable and interchangeable wheel models. The front hub bearing on the Light Solo models may be adjusted with the wheel in position.

Hub Lubrication. Grease gun nipples are provided for lubrication and the gun should be applied at least once every 1,000 miles. Use Wakefield's Castrolease Medium, Price's Belmoline "C," Esso Grease, Shell Retinax C.D., or Vacuum Mobilgrease No. 2.

Speedometer. The bevel gears in the speedometer gear-box should be lubricated every 500 miles with one of the greases mentioned above.

Decompressor. The larger models are fitted with a decompressor to provide easy starting and this is brought into operation by the handlebar lever. This operates a bell crank lever which presses on a sliding plunger in the exhaust cam. Adjustment for the decompressor control is provided and consists of an adjustor on the cable where it is attached to the bracket on the timing gear cover. The adjustment should be set so that the bell crank lever just makes contact with the plunger; if it bears hard on, excessive wear takes place and the decompressor will not function correctly. If any difficulty is experienced in operating the decompressor, lift the lever slightly and rock the machine in gear. This will have the effect of altering the valve positions, as should the engine come to rest at the beginning of the exhaust stroke the decompressor cam cannot be moved. As a general rule, a slightly larger throttle opening is necessary with the decompressor.

1939 O.H.V. MODELS

Removing Cylinder Head. First remove the petrol tank, the curburettor, the exhaust valve, the inlet-valve spring chamber cap, and the tappet-inspection cover. The bolt retaining the inlet rocker arm should be removed so that the special tool may be screwed into the rocker axle. After ascertaining that the inlet valve is closed, tap the special tool until the rocker arm is free and may be removed from its shaft. The ball cups from the long push-rods may be unscrewed and the rods lifted away. Undo several turns, the gland nut securing the push-rod cover tube to the crankcase. The exhaust-valve lifter should then be disconnected and the cable removed. Insert a spanner between the fourth and fifth cylinder fins, counting from the bottom of the barrel, and undo the four bolts securing the cylinder head to the barrel. If the cylinder head is lifted, it may be drawn away by rotating it about the cover-tube axis. Turn in a clockwise direction until the head is clear of the top tube. Keep the head in a horizontal position so that it clears the oil feed pipe inside the push-rod cover tube.

Valve Timing. Should the valve timing become deranged, the following procedure should be adopted. Remove the tappet-chamber cover in order to observe that the exhaust valve is just closing when the piston is on top dead centre. Take away the timing-case cover and remove the "Magdyno" driving-shaft sprocket bolts. Pull the "Magdyno" driving-shaft sprocket and the timing-gear camshaft sprocket outwards until both the sprockets can be removed, so that the chain may be taken away from the small chain sprocket. Care must be exercised not to rotate the "Magydno" armature shaft, as this will necessitate resetting the ignition timing. The 17-tooth timing-side engine pinion is secured to the shaft by two keys and a nut having a right-hand thread, the latter being locked in position by a tab washer. The "Magdyno" and camshaft chain wheels, each with 34 teeth, are secured to their shafts by five bolts, and before removing any of these it is advisable to mark the wheel and shaft with a line to ensure that the driving wheels are replaced in their original positions. An indelible pencil line or scratch with a sharp instrument across the shaft and wheel will serve.

When refitting the timing-gear chain, the chain should be placed on the small sprocket and connected with the camshaft wheel so that the scribed marks on the latter are in line with the scribed mark on the engine-shaft sprocket, and the centre of the "Magdyno" sprocket may then be engaged in the chain and lined up so that the scribed mark comes exactly opposite the line on the camshaft sprocket.

As the sprockets are marked in such a positive manner, it is a simple matter even for the novice to reset the valve timing. The engine should be rotated until the piston is at top dead centre and the camshaft inserted so that the cams are just bearing on their respective tappets, which should be indicated by the fact that the cam faces are at approximately 10 o'clock and 2 o'clock. Next fix the camshaft sprocket so that the scribed marks on it face the line on the engine-shaft sprocket and the centre of the "Magdyno" driving shaft. This will ensure that the sprocket is located in the correct position on the camshaft. The timing-gear chain, camshaft, and "Magdyno" sprockets may be refitted in the manner previously described. The correct valve timing is—

Inlet valve opens 25° before T.D.C. and closes 50° after B.D.C. Exhaust valve opens 65° before B.D.C. and closes 25° after T.D.C.

Removing Valves. After removing the cylinder head, take out the two screwed plugs on the left-hand side of the cylinder head and the cover plate over the exhaust-valve springs.

To remove the inlet valve and springs, first remove the bolt securing the rocker arm to its shaft with the aid of the special tubular spanner in the tool kit. By inserting the special tool and tapping so that the axle is driven to the right, the rocker arm may be removed together with the shaft. The valve is now accessible, and to compress the spring the special tool, consisting of a bar with two pointed screws in it, should be employed. Place the bar across the top face of the valve-spring chamber with the pointed screws engaging in the depressions cut in the valve-spring top cap. The two pointed screws should be evenly tightened down until the split-taper collet securing the spring to the valve can be removed, when the valve and spring may be removed. The bar is prevented from moving by the two small bolts which normally secure the aluminium cover over the valve-spring chamber. The pairs of valve springs are positioned by a mounting block, which is located by two dowel pins. Replacement is merely a reversal of

OVERHAULING

the above operations, but take care to refit the hardened valve-stem caps as these are sometimes liable to be overlooked.

Tappet Adjustment. The adjustment for valve clearance is provided by the screwed extensions on the long push-rods and is effected as follows: Remove the tappet cover and rotate the engine until the piston reaches top dead centre with both valves closed. Remove the inlet-valve rocker arm and push-rod so that access may be obtained to the exhaust valve. With the tappet spanner, hold the hexagon on the push-rod (Fig. 60) and loosen the lock-nut B. Screw the head A in or out until the clearance is nil, i.e. it should be possible to just rotate the push-rods freely without any up-and-down movement. After the inlet rocker and push-rod are replaced, the same procedure should be adopted. It is unnecessary to use force when tightening the rocker adjustment cover.

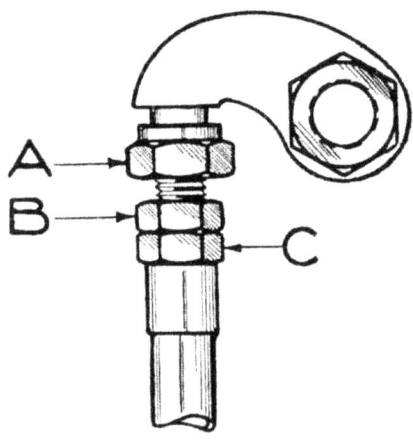

FIG. 60. TAPPET ADJUSTMENT ON 1939 O.H.V. MODELS

Clutch Adjustment. It is essential that there should be about $\frac{1}{2}$ in. free movement on the handlebar lever, measured at the tip. Adjustment is provided at the clutch-cable stop, which is threaded into the kick-starter casing. To take up play between the control and the thrust rod, the adjuster should be unscrewed from the kick-starter case cover.

Lubricating Control Wires. Efficient control of the machine can only be obtained if the control cables work smoothly, and with this object in mind the makers have ingeniously provided a method of lubrication, which consists of small metal clips covering bare patches on the outer casings. The clips can be slipped aside and the nozzle of a specially constructed oil-gun applied. This gun is clamped to the casing, pressure being applied by a large milled-edge disk under a rubber pad, and oil is forced through the metal spiral of the outer casing by turning the screwed plunger of the gun in a clockwise direction.

INDEX

ADJUSTING chains, 16
—— clutch, 60
—— front and rear hubs, 70
Amal needle jet carburettor, 80

BATTERY maintenance, 95
Big end renewal, 43
Braking, 7
Brushes, dynamo, 88

CARBURETTOR, 32, 79, 108
Choice of lubricants, 19
Clubs, 5
Clutch adjustment, 60, 116
Commutators, 90
Competitions and competition work, 104
Components, 67
Cornering, 7
Cycle parts, 18, 109

DECARBONIZING, 30, 116
Dismantling clutch, 63
—— engine, 42
—— gear-box, 53
Driving, 8
Dry sump lubrication, 21
Dynamo, 88

ELECTRICAL systems, 88
Engine, how it works, 27

FOCUSING headlamp bulb, 93
Four-stroke cycle, 28

GEAR-BOX and clutch, 52
Grinding-in valves, 37, 115

HINTS for the detection and remedy of faults, 96
Hubs, adjusting, 70, 120

INSURANCE, 1

KICK-STARTER mechanism, 65

LAMPS, 3
Lubrication, 19

MAGNETO timing, 50
Maintenance of a new machine, 16
—— of the Amal carburettor, 87
—— —— magneto, 101

NUMBER plates, 3

PILLION riding, 8
Piston removal, 33
—— rings, 34

REGISTRATION book, 3
Reliability trials, 106
Removal of divided rear axle wheel, 71
Removing carbon, 35
—— carburettor, 32
—— cylinder, 33
—— valves, 37
Road signs, 11
Rocker-box and rockers, 40
Running-in, 5

SPARKING plug, cleaning, etc., 76
Speed events, 107

TAIL lamp, 94
Tappets, 17, 123
Testing condition of battery, 95
Tyres, 75, 112

USE of clutch, 6

VALVE gear, 48, 108
—— guides, 114

WHEELS, removal, 69
Wiring of the equipment, 90

AUTOBOOKS WORKSHOP MANUALS

ALFA ROMEO GIULIA 1300, 1600, 1750, 2000 1962-1978 WSM
BMW 1600 1966-1973 WSM
BMW 2000 & 2002 1966-1976 WSM
BMW 2500, 2800, 3.0 & 3.3 1968-1977 WSM
BMW 316, 320, 320i 1975-1977 WSM
BMW 518, 520, 520i 1973-1981 WSM
FIAT 1100, 1100D, 1100R & 1200 1957-1969 WSM
FIAT 124 1966-1974 WSM
FIAT 124 SPORT 1966-1975 WSM
FIAT 125 & 125 SPECIAL 1967-1973 WSM
FIAT 126, 126L, 126 DV, 126/650 & 126/650 DV 1972-1982 WSM
FIAT 127 SALOON, SPECIAL & SPORT, 900, 1050 1971-1981 WSM
FIAT 128 1969-1982 WSM
FIAT 1300, 1500 1961-1967 WSM
FIAT 131 MIRAFIORI 1975-1982 WSM
FIAT 132 1972-1982 WSM
FIAT 500 1957-1973 WSM
FIAT 600, 600D & MULTIPLA 1955-1969 WSM
FIAT 850 1964-1972 WSM
JAGUAR E-TYPE 1961-1972 WSM
JAGUAR MK 1, 2 1955-1969 WSM
JAGUAR S TYPE, 420 1963-1968 WSM
JAGUAR XK 120, 140, 150 MK 7, 8, 9 1948-1961 WSM
LAND ROVER 1, 2 1948-1961 WSM
MERCEDES-BENZ 190 1959-1968 WSM
MERCEDES-BENZ 220/8 1968-1972 WSM
MERCEDES-BENZ 220B 1959-1965 WSM
MERCEDES-BENZ 230 1963-1968 WSM
MERCEDES-BENZ 250 1968-1972 WSM
MERCEDES-BENZ 280 1968-1972 WSM
MG MIDGET TA-TF 1936-1955 WSM
MINI 1959-1980 WSM
MORRIS MINOR 1952-1971 WSM
PEUGEOT 404 1960-1975 WSM
PORSCHE 911 1964-1973 WSM
PORSCHE 911 1970-1977 WSM
RENAULT 16 1965-1979 WSM
RENAULT 8, 10, 1100 1962-1971 WSM
ROVER 3500, 3500S 1968-1976 WSM
SUNBEAM RAPIER, ALPINE 1955-1965 WSM
TRIUMPH SPITFIRE, GT6, VITESSE 1962-1968 WSM
TRIUMPH TR2, TR3, TR3A 1952-1962 WSM
TRIUMPH TR4, TR4A 1961-1967 WSM
VOLKSWAGEN BEETLE 1968-1977 WSM

VELOCEPRESS AUTOMOBILE BOOKS & MANUALS

ABARTH BUYERS GUIDE
AUSTIN-HEALEY 6-CYLINDER WSM
AUSTIN-HEALEY SPRITE & MG MIDGET 1958-1971 WSM
BMW 600 LIMOUSINE FACTORY WSM
BMW 600 LIMOUSINE OWNERS HAND BOOK & SERVICE MANUAL
BMW ISETTA FACTORY WSM
BOOK OF THE CARRERA PANAMERICANA - MEXICAN ROAD RACE
COMPLETE CATALOG OF JAPANESE MOTOR VEHICLES
CORVAIR 1960-1969 OWNERS WORKSHOP MANUAL
CORVETTE V8 1955-1962 OWNERS WORKSHOP MANUAL
DIALED IN - THE JAN OPPERMAN STORY
FERRARI 250/GT SERVICE AND MAINTENANCE
FERRARI 308 SERIES BUYER'S AND OWNER'S GUIDE
FERRARI BERLINETTA LUSSO
FERRARI BROCHURES AND SALES LITERATURE 1946-1967
FERRARI BROCHURES AND SALES LITERATURE 1968-1989
FERRARI GUIDE TO PERFORMANCE
FERRARI OPP, MAINTENANCE & SERVICE H/BOOKS 1948-1963
FERRARI OWNER'S HANDBOOK
FERRARI SERIAL NUMBERS PART I - ODD NUMBERS TO 21399
FERRARI SERIAL NUMBERS PART II - EVEN NUMBERS TO 1050
FERRARI SPYDER CALIFORNIA
FERRARI TUNING TIPS & MAINTENANCE TECHNIQUES
HENRY'S FABULOUS MODEL "A" FORD
HOW TO BUILD A FIBERGLASS CAR
HOW TO BUILD A RACING CAR
HOW TO RESTORE THE MODEL 'A' FORD
IF HEMINGWAY HAD WRITTEN A RACING NOVEL
JAGUAR E-TYPE 3.8 & 4.2 WSM
LE MANS 24 (THE BOOK THAT THE FILM WAS BASED ON)
MASERATI BROCHURES AND SALES LITERATURE
MASERATI OWNER'S HANDBOOK
METROPOLITAN FACTORY WSM
MGA & MGB OWNERS HANDBOOK & WSM
OBERT'S FIAT GUIDE
PERFORMANCE TUNING THE SUNBEAM TIGER
PORSCHE 356 1948-1965 WSM
PORSCHE 912 WSM
SOUPING THE VOLKSWAGEN
TRIUMPH TR2, TR3, TR4 1953-1965 WSM
TUNING FOR SPEED (P.E. IRVING)
VEDA ORR'S NEW REVISED HOT ROD PICTORIAL
VOLKSWAGEN TRANSPORTER, TRUCKS, STATION WAGONS WSM
VOLVO 1944-1968 ALL MODELS WSM
WEBER CARBURETORS (EMPHASIS ON ALFA & FIAT)

BROOKLANDS BOOKS & ROAD TEST PORTFOLIOS (RTP)

AC CARS 1904-2009
ALFA ROMEO 1920-1933 ROAD TEST PORTFOLIO
ALFA ROMEO 1934-1940 ROAD TEST PORTFOLIO
BRABHAM RALT HONDA THE RON TAURANAC STORY
BUGATTI TYPE 10 TO TYPE 40 ROAD TEST PORTFOLIO
BUGATTI TYPE 10 TO TYPE 251 ROAD TEST PORTFOLIO
BUGATTI TYPE 41 TO TYPE 55 ROAD TEST PORTFOLIO
BUGATTI TYPE 57 TO TYPE 251 ROAD TEST PORTFOLIO
DELAHAYE ROAD TEST PORTFOLIO
FERRARI ROAD CARS 1946-1956 ROAD TEST PORTFOLIO
FIAT 500 1936-1972 ROAD TEST PORTFOLIO
FIAT DINO ROAD TEST PORTFOLIO
HISPANO SUIZA ROAD TEST PORTFOLIO
HONDA ST1100/ST1300 PAN EUROPEAN 1990-2002 RTP
JAGUAR MK1 & MK2 ROAD TEST PORTFOLIO
LOTUS CORTINA ROAD TEST PORTFOLIO
MV AGUSTA F4 750 & 1000 1997-2007 ROAD TEST PORTFOLIO
TATRA CARS ROAD TEST PORTFOLIO

VELOCEPRESS MOTORCYCLE BOOKS & MANUALS

AJS SINGLES & TWINS 250cc THRU 1000cc 1932-1948 (BOOK OF)
AJS SINGLES 1955-65 350cc & 500cc (BOOK OF)
AJS SINGLES 1945-60 350cc & 500cc MODELS 16 & 18 (BOOK OF)
ARIEL 1939-1960 4 STROKE SINGLES (BOOK OF)
ARIEL LEADER & ARROW 1958-1964 (BOOK OF)
ARIEL MOTORCYCLES 1933-1951 WSM
ARIEL PREWAR MODELS 1932-1939 (BOOK OF)
BMW M/CYCLES R26 R27 (1956-1967) FACTORY WSM
BMW M/CYCLES R50 R50S R60 R69S (1955-1969) FACTORY WSM
BSA BANTAM (BOOK OF)
BSA ALL FOUR-STROKE SINGLES & V-TWINS 1936-1952 (BOOK OF)
BSA OHV & SV SINGLES - 250cc 1954-1970 (BOOK OF)
BSA OHV & SV SINGLES 1945-54 250-600cc (BOOK OF)
BSA OHV SINGLES 350 & 500cc 1955-1967 (BOOK OF)
BSA PRE-WAR MODELS TO 1939 (BOOK OF)
BSA TWINS 1948-1962 (BOOK OF)
BSA TWINS 1962-1969 (SECOND BOOK OF)
CATALOG OF BRITISH MOTORCYCLES (1951 MODELS)
DOUGLAS PRE-WAR ALL MODELS 1929-1939 (BOOK OF)
DOUGLAS POST-WAR ALL MODELS 1948-1957 FACTORY WSM
DUCATI 160cc, 250cc & 350cc OHC MODELS FACTORY WSM
HONDA 50 ALL MODELS UP TO 1970 INC MONKEY & TRAIL (BOOK OF)
HONDA 90 ALL MODELS UP TO 1966 (BOOK OF)
HONDA MOTORCYCLES 125-150 TWINS C/CS/CB/CA WSM
HONDA MOTORCYCLES 250-305 TWINS C/CS/CB WSM
HONDA MOTORCYCLES C100 SUPER CUB WSM
HONDA MOTORCYCLES C110 SPORT CUB 1962-1969 WSM
HONDA TWINS & SINGLES 50cc THRU 305cc 1960-1966 (BOOK OF)
HONDA TWINS ALL MODELS 125cc THRU 450cc UP TO 1968 (BOOK OF)
INDIAN PONYBIKE, BOY RACER & PAPOOSE ILL PARTS LIST & SALES LIT
LAMBRETTA ALL 125 & 150cc MODELS 1947-1957 (BOOK OF)
LAMBRETTA LI & TV MODELS 1957-1970 (SECOND BOOK OF)
MATCHLESS 350 & 500cc SINGLES 1945-1956 (BOOK OF)
MATCHLESS 350 & 500cc SINGLES 1955-1966 (BOOK OF)
NORTON 1932-1947 (BOOK OF)
NORTON 1938-1956 (BOOK OF)
NORTON DOMINATOR TWINS 1955-1965 (BOOK OF)
NORTON MODELS 19, 50 & ES2 1955-1963 (BOOK OF)
NORTON MOTORCYCLES 1957-1970 FACTORY WSM
NORTON PREWAR MODELS 1932-1939 (BOOK OF)
NSU QUICKLY ALL MODELS 1953-1963 (BOOK OF)
RALEIGH MOPEDS 1960-1969 (BOOK OF)
ROYAL ENFIELD SINGLES & V TWINS 1937-1953 (BOOK OF)
ROYAL ENFIELD SINGLES 1946-1962 (BOOK OF)
ROYAL ENFIELD 736cc INTERCEPTOR FACTORY WSM
ROYAL ENFIELD 250cc & 350cc SINGLES 1958-1966 (SECOND BOOK OF)
SUNBEAM MOTORCYCLES 1928-1939 (BOOK OF)
SUNBEAM S7 & S8 1946-1957 (BOOK OF)
SUZUKI 50cc & 80cc UP TO 1966 (BOOK OF)
SUZUKI T10 1963-1967 FACTORY WSM
SUZUKI T20 & T200 1965-1969 FACTORY WSM
TRIUMPH PRE-WAR MOTORCYCLE 1935-1939 (BOOK OF)
TRIUMPH MOTORCYCLES 1937-1951 WSM
TRIUMPH MOTORCYCLES 1945-1955 FACTORY WSM
TRIUMPH TWINS 1956-1969 (BOOK OF)
VELOCETTE ALL SINGLES & TWINS 1925-1970 (BOOK OF)
VESPA 1951-1961 (BOOK OF)
VESPA 125 & 150cc & GS MODELS 1955-1963 (SECOND BOOK OF)
VESPA 90, 125 & 150cc 1963-1972 (THIRD BOOK OF)
VESPA GS & SS 1955-1968 (BOOK OF)
VILLIERS ENGINE (BOOK OF)
VINCENT MOTORCYCLES 1935-1955 WSM

**PLEASE VISIT OUR WEBSITE
www.VelocePress.com
FOR A DETAILED DESCRIPTION
OF ANY OF THESE TITLES**

Please check our website:

www.VelocePress.com

for a complete up-to-date list of available titles

www.ingramcontent.com/pod-product-compliance
Lightning Source LLC
Chambersburg PA
CBHW070555170426

43201CB00012B/1846